THE COMPLETE WOK COOKBOOK

140 Easy Recipes For Cooking At Home Tasty Asian Food

By

Maki Blanc

WOK
COOKBOOK

70 Easy Recipes for Traditional Asian Food

By

Maki Blanc

© Copyright 2021 by Maki Blanc - All rights reserved.

This document is geared towards providing exact and reliable information in regard to the topic and issue covered. The publication is sold with the idea that the publisher is not required to render accounting, officially permitted, or otherwise, qualified services. If advice is necessary, legal or professional, a practiced individual in the profession should be ordered.

From a Declaration of Principles which was accepted and approved equally by a Committee of the American Bar Association and a Committee of Publishers and Associations.

In no way is it legal to reproduce, duplicate, or transmit any part of this document in either electronic means or in printed format. Recording of this publication is strictly prohibited and any storage of this document is not allowed unless with written permission from the publisher. All rights reserved.

The information provided herein is stated to be truthful and consistent, in that any liability, in terms of inattention or otherwise, by any usage or abuse of any policies, processes, or directions contained within is the solitary and utter responsibility of the recipient reader. Under no circumstances will any legal responsibility or blame be held against the publisher for any reparation, damages, or monetary loss due to the information herein, either directly or indirectly.

Respective authors own all copyrights not held by the publisher.

The information herein is offered for informational purposes solely and is universal as so. The presentation of the information is without contract or any type of guarantee assurance.

The trademarks that are used are without any consent, and the publication of the trademark is without permission or backing by the trademark owner. All trademarks and brands within this book are for clarifying purposes only and are owned by the owners themselves, not affiliated with this document.

Contents

INTRODUCTION 13

CHAPTER 1: INTRODUCTION TO THE WOK COOKING 14

1.1 History and Origin of Wok 14

1.2 History of Traditional Wok Dishes 15

1.3 Evolution of Wok Cooking over Time 16

1.4 Wok Foods According to Nutrition and Dietetics 17

1.5 Key Ingredients Used in the Wok Recipes 18

CHAPTER 2: THE WORLD OF TRADITIONAL WOK BREAKFAST RECIPES 22

2.1 Wok Breakfast Fried Rice Recipe 22

2.2 Wok Bacon and Egg Fried Rice Recipe 23

2.3 Wok Breakfast Omelet Recipe 25

2.4 Wok Breakfast Fried Egg Recipe 26

2.5 Wok Tomato and Egg Stir-Fry Recipe 27

2.6 Wok Scrambled Egg with Salmon Recipe 28

2.7 Wok Meat Breakfast Hash Recipe 29

2.8 Wok Shashuka Recipe 30

2.9 Wok Cinnamon Omelet Recipe 31

2.10 Wok Crispy Breakfast Rice Recipe 32

2.11 Wok Spicy Omelet Recipe 33

2.12 Wok Southwest Tofu Scramble Recipe 34

CHAPTER 3: THE WORLD OF TRADITIONAL WOK LUNCH RECIPES 36

3.1 Wok Chicken Stir-Fry Recipe 36

3.2 Wok Seared Chicken and Vegetables Recipe 37

3.3 Wok Seared Scallops with Tangerine Sauce Recipe 38

3.4 Wok Stir Cod with Stir-Fried Mushrooms Recipe 40

3.5 Wok Beef Stir-Fry Recipe 41

3.6 Wok Kung Pao Chicken Recipe 42

3.7 Wok Ginger Sesame Tofu Recipe 44

3.8 Wok Teriyaki Tofu Rice Recipe 45

3.9 Wok Creamy Tomato Pasta Recipe 46

3.10 Wok Kung Pao Shrimp Recipe 48

3.11 Wok Chicken Sausage and Vegetable Curry Recipe 49

3.12 Wok Crispy Tofu and Vegetable Stir-Fry Recipe 50

3.13 Wok Shredded Pork with Crispy Tofu Recipe 52

3.14 Wok Sweet and Sour Chicken Recipe 53

3.15 Wok Mongolian Beef and Broccoli Recipe 55

3.16 Wok Coconut Curry Noodle Soup Recipe 56

3.17 Wok Crispy Tofu in Ginger and Garlic Sauce Recipe 57

3.18 Wok Beef and Mushroom Stew Recipe 58

CHAPTER 4: THE WORLD OF TRADITIONAL WOK DINNER RECIPES 61

4.1 Wok Black Pepper Chicken Recipe 61

4.2 Wok Thai Chili Basil Chicken Recipe 62

4.3 Wok Spicy Chicken with Peanuts Recipe 63

4.4 Wok Beef with Broccoli and Oyster Sauce Recipe 65

4.5 Wok Spicy Chicken and Leek Stir-Fry Recipe 66

4.6 Wok Almond and Vegetable Stir-Fry Recipe 67

4.7 Wok Sweet and Sour Beef Recipe 68

4.8 Wok Turkey and Asparagus Stir-Fry Recipe 70

4.9 Wok Coconut and Shrimp Curry Recipe 71

4.10 Wok Mandarin Pork Stir-Fry Recipe 72

4.11 Wok Scallops and Asparagus Stir-Fry Recipe 73

4.12 Wok Mexican Steak Stir-Fry Recipe 74

4.13 Wok Orange and Beef Stir-Fry Recipe 76

4.14 Wok Chicken Soba Noodles Recipe 77

4.15 Wok Pineapple Fried Rice Recipe 78

CHAPTER 5: THE WORLD OF TRADITIONAL WOK DESSERT RECIPES 80

5.1 Wok Stir-Fried Bananas Foster Recipe 80

5.2 Wok Stir-Fried Apples Shortcake Recipe 81

5.3 Wok Steamed Red Bean Bun Recipe 82

5.4 Wok Steamed Coconut Bun Recipe 83

5.5 Wok Sesame Balls Recipe 86

5.6 Wok Snow Skin Mooncakes Recipe 87

5.7 Wok Steamed White Sugar Sponge Cake Recipe................88

5.8 Wok Peach Squares Recipe 89

5.9 Wok Snow Fungus Soup with Pears Recipe 90

5.10 Wok Apple Cinnamon Coffee Cake Recipe 91

5.11 Wok Mango Sago Recipe 92

5.12 Wok Golden Syrup Recipe 93

5.13 Wok Egg Tarts Recipe..94

5.14 Wok Banana Bread Recipe 95

5.15 Wok Sweet Rice Balls with Black Sesame Filling Recipe ..96

CHAPTER 6: THE WORLD OF TRADITIONAL WOK RECIPES EATEN ONLY BY THAI PEOPLE 98

6.1 Wok Cabbage Burji Recipe...98

6.2 Wok Breakfast Poha Recipe 99

6.3 Wok Simple Millet Congee Recipe 100

6.4 Wok Osmanthus Cake Recipe..103

6.5 Wok Chinese Sweet Peanut Cream Dessert Recipe.............104

6.6 Wok Sichuan Chicken and Vegetables Recipe 105

6.7 Wok Siri Lankan Spicy Breakfast Omelet Recipe 106

6.8 Wok Chinese Chili Chicken Dry Recipe 108

6.9 Wok Mongolian Chicken Recipe 109

6.10 Wok Chinese Omelet Recipe 110

CONCLUSION 112

CHAPTER 1: VEGETARIAN WOK INDIAN RECIPES 117

1.1 Indian Five-Spice Vegetable Stir-Fry 117

1.2 Wok-Seared Vegetables 118

1.3 Noodles and Vegetables Stir Fry 119

1.4 Indian Stir-Fried Carrots 120

1.5 Vegetables in Hot Garlic Sauce 121

1.6 Stir-Fried Exotic Oriental Vegetable Recipe 122

1.7 Potato and Green Beans Stir Fry 123

1.8 Balti Stir-Fried Vegetables with Cashews 124

1.9 Stir-Fried Indian Okra with Spices 125

1.10 Vegetable Jalfrezi 126

1.11 Quinoa Fried Rice Recipe 127

1.12 Chili Paneer 129

1.13 Frozen Mixed Vegetable Fry 130

1.14 Curry Fried Rice 131

1.15 South Indian Brinjal Stir Fry 132

1.16 Indian-Spiced Pickled Vegetables 133

1.17 Cashew Chickpea Curry 135

1.18 Stir-Fried Chili Greens 136

CHAPTER 2: VEGETARIAN WOK JAPANESE RECIPES 138

2.1 Yasai Itame **138**

2.2 Japanese Stir-Fried Noodles with Veggies **139**

2.3 Lightly Fried Japanese Vegetables **140**

2.4 Vegan Stir-Fried Udon Noodles **141**

2.5 Vegetable Yakisoba **142**

2.6 Hibachi Vegetables **143**

2.7 Wagamama Wok-Fried Greens **144**

2.8 Vegan Mapo Nasu **144**

2.9 15 Minute Spicy Udon Stir Fry **145**

2.10 Stir-Fried Tofu with Vegetables **147**

2.11 Japanese Mushroom Stir-Fry **148**

2.12 Veggie Stir-Fry Soba Noodle **149**

2.13 Speedy Japanese Miso Stir Fry & Sticky Rice **151**

2.14 Japanese Shrimp & Eggplant Fried Rice **153**

2.15 Vegan Ramen **153**

2.16 Vegetable Lo Mein **155**

2.17 Szechuan Eggplant **156**

CHAPTER 3: VEGETARIAN WOK CHINESE RECIPES.158

3.1 Saucy Vegetable Stir Fry **158**

3.2 Vegetable Stir-Fry Noodles **159**

3.3 Ginger Veggie Stir Fry 159

3.4 Stir-Fried Lettuce with Garlic Chiles 160

3.5 Wok Black Bean Glaze and Tossed Veggies in Honey Recipe ..161

3.6 Shrimp and Chinese Vegetable Stir-Fry 162

3.7 Black Bean Sauce with Stir Fry Veggies 163

3.8 Spring Veggie Stir-Fry 164

3.9 Chinese Cabbage Stir-Fry 165

3.10 Veggie and Tofu Stir-Fry 166

3.11 Seitan Stir-Fry and Vegan Chinese Vegetable Recipe 167

3.12 Tofu Stir-Fry with Garlic Sauce 168

3.13 Chinese Broccoli with Oyster Sauce 169

3.14 Ramen Stir Fry 170

3.15 Chinese Fried Rice 172

3.16 Cashew Stir Fry Kale Mushroom 173

3.17 Vegetables in Hot Garlic Sauce 173

3.18 Stir-Fried Chinese Egg Noodles with Oyster Sauce 175

CHAPTER 4: VEGETARIAN WOK THAI RECIPES 177

4.1 Thai Stir-Fried Vegetables with Garlic, Ginger, and Lime 177

4.2 Thai Stir-Fried Mixed Vegetables Recipe 179

4.3 Vegetarian Thai Noodles 180

4.4 Easy Thai Basil Vegetable Stir Fry 181

4.5 Spicy Thai Basil Fried Rice 182

4.6 Thai Vegetable Fried Rice with Cashews **183**

4.7 Vegetarian Thai Yellow Curry..**184**

4.8 Thai Satay Stir-Fry **185**

4.9 Vegetarian Pad See Ew with Tofu and Chinese Eggplant..........**186**

4.10 Veggie Thai Red Curry...**187**

4.11 Easy Vegetable Stir Fry with Creamy Peanut Sauce **188**

4.12 Thai Morning Glory Stir Fry **190**

4.13 Thai Combination Fried Rice **190**

4.14 Vegetarian Pad Thai with Zoodles..**191**

4.15 Thai Stir-Fry with Coconut Rice..**193**

4.16 Thai Green Curry with Homemade Curry Paste.......................**195**

4.17 Rainbow Vegetarian Pad Thai with Crispy Noodles **195**

CONCLUSION **197**

Introduction

Cooking is a beautiful and mesmerizing art that has been performed from the beginning of civilization. Humans have used various shapes and sizes of utensils to prepare their food. The wok has been in the cooking field since the time of Chinese traditions. People used wok as a utensil that could help them cook large amount of food in a comparatively short time.

The wok is acknowledged to have first been made in China, over 2000 years in the period of the Han custom. The name "Wok" has been extricated from the Cantonese word meaning "Cooking Pot." The early models of the wok were made of cast iron metals, allowing them to be stronger and more solid.

This book deals with the wok cooking. You will learn the detail about the history of wok dishes and the evolution of wok dishes with respect to time. The wok does not only cook the food for you but also preserves the healthy minerals, vitamins and other nutritious agents that usually die due to intense cooking. There are various key ingredients that you need before starting to cook your food in the wok.

There are various health benefits of having a wok at home and using it as a cooking utensil. You will learn all of these benefits when you go through the different properties of cooking using a wok. You will get over 70 different breakfast, lunch, dinner, and dessert, and authentic recipes that are only eaten by Asian people. You can easily start cooking at home with the detailed instructions present below each recipe. So start reading and start cooking today.

Chapter 1: Introduction to the Wok Cooking

Wok is a flimsy walled cooking container, molded like a shallow bowl with handles. It is broadly utilized in Chinese-style cooking. The wok has a round base that concentrates heat, preparing food rapidly with generally very little oil.

Food when prepared might be thrown to the inclining side of the wok to remain warm without cooking further, while other food is prepared at the base of the wok. The wok was developed as a device to conserve scarce oil. It is for the most part made of iron, copper, carbon steel, or aluminum.

From streak cooked sautés to hand beaten servings of blended greens, wok serves as an effective cooking utensil. If you value eating, you will be in a paradise with the combination and variety of food in this cooking style.

1.1 History and Origin of Wok

As mentioned before, wok is acknowledged to have first been made in China, over 2000 years in the period of the Han custom. Food specialists have various speculations with respect to why the wok was developed. Some state that because of the deficiency of food back in the Han tradition, the wok took into consideration for a wide assortment of suppers to be cooked utilizing similar fixings because of its adaptability.

There is also a theory that many years ago, due to different clans travelling across the country and having to carry all their belongings with them. They needed a utensil that was not only portable but also able to quickly cook large amounts of food to feed the clan.

A third hypothesis is that because of a lack of fuel and oil in the Han line, the wok took into account individuals to prepare dinners utilizing next to no oil. You will learn from the different recipes in the book below that you possibly need a limited quantity of vegetable oil when utilizing a wok at home to cook your meals.

Nowadays, wok is utilized everywhere in the world for an entire scope of various meals. Most of the woks are produced using carbon steel, which is considered to be a strong material and non-sticky in nature. Obviously, preparing Asian food depends intensely on the wok, yet there are numerous dishes that can be made using the wok.

1.2 History of Traditional Wok Dishes

With a long history, remarkable highlights, various styles and lovely cooking, wok dishes are one significant constituent piece of Chinese culture. Traditional wok dishes are well known for its shading, smell, taste, and appearance.

Stir-frying is a strategy for cooking that is the mainly uses a wok. Wok traditional dishes included only stir-fried dishes. It includes the utilization of dry heat to the food, which is cooked in a little amount of hot oil, while being persistently blended all through the cycle.

Stir-frying is generally polished in Asia, and famous plans for Chow Mein, fried rice and lettuce wraps are exceptionally in mainstream across the globe.

Stir Frying originated in China as two separate methods, Chao and Bao. The methods differed on the basis of the Time of cooking, intensity of heat and amount of tossing involved. Stir Fried recipes started spreading from China to the entire Asian continent as stir frying imparted a delectable flavor to the dishes prepared using this method.

A round lined container called a Wok was customarily used to make sautéed dishes, which is as yet utilized for preparing the vast majority of these plans, particularly in terrain China. Noodles and rice, which are the staples in the Chinese food, are generally cooked by this particular method.

Sautéing is a technique frequently mistook for stir frying, as the two strategies include broiling and throwing the ingredients in hot oil. Sautéing is a French method completed on a skillet on generally low warmth, though stir-frying is a Chinese strategy, which is done on a wok put on extremely high warmth.

1.3 Evolution of Wok Cooking over Time

Traditionally, the wok was created to cook food in a large quantity for many people. Currently the wok is used to enhance the flavor of a particular dish and to cook any particular dish very quickly within a few minutes.

The wok has not evolved with Time with respect to its shape, though the handles have gone through changes into various types. The dishes and techniques of cooking used while cooking in a wok have changed enormously. Now, many cooks use woks for many types of cooking rather than just stir-fried cooking. Wok is now used for sautéing, frying, stew making, making soups and many other cooking methods.

1.4 Wok Foods According to Nutrition and Dietetics

Wok cooking, likewise called sautéing can be a sound method to set up your dinners, particularly in the event that you use a lot of vegetables in your dish. This is just the situation, nonetheless, in the event that you limit the quantity of high-sodium and high-fat elements and do not add a great deal of oil or fat during the cooking process.

When stir-frying foods, you only need a minimal amount of oil due to the high heat used in this cooking method. You can even replace the fat with broth to lower the final fat content of your meal even more. You will want to include at least a small amount of fat, either from the oil used to stir-fry your food or in the form of meat or nuts because otherwise you will not be able to absorb all of the fat-soluble vitamins from the vegetables in the dish.

Eating meals that to a great extent involve non-bland veggies and furthermore contain protein and fat can assist you with keeping up stable glucose levels for the duration of the day.

This, thusly, prompts supported energy and may help weight reduction. Curries, wok-sears, and soups are made with an assortment of vegetables, incorporate a protein source like tofu, lean meat, or fish, and contain coconut milk, nut sauces, or other fat.

Long cooking times increase the loss of heat-sensitive vitamins, including vitamin C and the B vitamin thiamine. Quickly stir-frying vegetables in a small amount of oil helps minimize these losses. Although the high temperatures used will still cause some nutrient losses. But these losses would be much more if you grilled baked or roasted your food rather than cooking it in a wok, because of the much shorter cooking time.

Every time you cook, you have a choice of preparation methods. Some methods are healthier than others. The choices you make when cooking, influence the total calories in the meal and the nutritional benefits, and these choices can affect your health. Switching from unhealthy to healthy cooking methods is an easy, beneficial change to make.

1.5 Key Ingredients Used in the Wok Recipes

A large portion of the ingredients found in Wok cooking are a clear reflection of the environment warm, fertile land and abundant water. Recipes depend on fish, outlandish products of the soil, a few sorts of noodles and sauces. Rice is the mainstay of most meals, giving an ideal equality to the wide grouping of tastes and tones that envelop it. Hot flavoring mixes are utilized to season everything from the day's catch to the easy to make servings of rice or noodles. Following are a portion of the primary ingredients utilized in wok cooking:

- White peppercorns: Wok cooks broil fragrant, natural peppercorn seed in a dry container to draw out its flavor, and afterward granulate it for use in curry pastes and other zest mixes. White peppercorn is likewise an essential fixing in many flavor mixes, soups, stews, meat, bean and rice dishes.

- Basil: Basil is utilized both as an enhancing flavor and a topping in wok cooking Small bunch are here and there used in soups, curries and sautés prior to serving.

- Garlic: Wok cooks use garlic for its health properties, fragrance, and the way that its flavor mixes well with an assortment of different flavors.

- Cardamom: The fragrant cardamom seedpod is utilized in a couple of wok dishes of Indian inception. Somewhat lemony, cardamom additionally has a marginally peppery and sweet taste as well as fragrance.

- Soy sauce: The light, lemony flavor and aroma of soy sauce is a staple in wok food. Thai cooks utilize the bulb and base leaves of lemongrass to prepare sauces, soups, wok-sears and curries. It improves the taste of meats, poultry, fish, and vegetables, and it is particularly delicious with garlic, chilies and cilantro.

- Sesame oil: Its flavor is sweet, warm, and somewhat peppery. However, it is utilized principally for shading in numerous wok dishes, including curries, toppings, fish and grain dishes.

- Curry Powders and Pastes: Thais generally mix their own curry powders and pastes by pounding different spices and flavors in a mortar and pestle. Curries are utilized to season coconut milk, serving of mixed greens dressings, noodle sauces, fish and meat dishes, vegetable dishes and soups.

- Hot sauce: Wok food is hot, because of the generous utilization of new and dried stew peppers in the form of hot sauce. Despite the fact that hot sauces are not local, they are presently fundamental for wok cooking.

- Ginger: The strongly fragrant and somewhat interesting kind of ginger root is valued in wok cooking. Thai cooks utilize the root and the leaf of the plant.

- Mace: It is somewhat nutty, and its warm taste is found in soups, stuffing, sauces and heated products. It supplements fish, meats, and cheddar, just as certain refreshments.

- Cilantro: Also known as Chinese parsley and cooks utilize this delicate, verdant plant for its unique flavor and natural or amazing fragrance.

- Nutmeg: Wok cooks appreciate the extreme fragrance and sweet, zesty kind of nutmeg in the recipes of sweet and appetizing dishes. The cooks utilize a machine to finely powder the nutmeg.

Wok cooking will engage any cook who adores the art of seasoning. And while many dishes are very hot, those prepared at home can be adjusted to just the right degree for your own tastes.

Chapter 2: The World of Traditional Wok Breakfast Recipes

Following are some classic traditional wok breakfast recipes that are rich in healthy nutrients and you can easily make them with the detailed instructions list in each recipe:

2.1 Wok Breakfast Fried Rice Recipe

Preparation Time: 30 minutes
Cooking Time: 10 minutes
Serving: 4

Ingredients:

- Red chilies, two
- Jalapeno, one large
- Sliced green onions, half cup
- White peppercorns, one teaspoon
- Cilantro, one cup
- Fresh ginger, one teaspoon
- Fish sauce, one tablespoon
- Soy sauce, one tablespoon
- Chinese 5 spice, half teaspoon
- Chili garlic sauce, two tablespoon
- Fresh cilantro leaves, half cup
- Fresh basil leaves, a quarter cup
- Chicken broth, one can
- Minced lemon grass, one teaspoon
- Egg, one large
- Cooked rice, as required

Instructions:
1. Add all the ingredients of the curry into a wok.
2. Add the chicken broth and sauces into the mixture.
3. Cook your dish for ten minutes.
4. Add the cooked rice into the mixture.
5. Mix the rice well and cook it for five minutes.
6. Add eggs into the wok by pushing the rest of the ingredients to a side.
7. Cook the egg and then mix the rest of the ingredients into it.
8. Cook your dish for five more minutes.
9. Add the cilantro into the dish.
10. Mix your rice and then dish it out.
11. Your dish is ready to be served.

2.2 Wok Bacon and Egg Fried Rice Recipe

Preparation Time: 30 minutes
Cooking Time: 10 minutes
Serving: 4

Ingredients:

- Red chilies, two
- Jalapeno, one large
- Sliced green onions, half cup
- White peppercorns, one teaspoon
- Cilantro, one cup
- Fresh ginger, one teaspoon
- Fish sauce, one tablespoon
- Soy sauce, one tablespoon
- Chinese 5 spice, half teaspoon

- Chili garlic sauce, two tablespoon
- Fresh cilantro leaves, half cup
- Fresh basil leaves, a quarter cup
- Chicken broth, one can
- Minced lemon grass, one teaspoon
- Egg, one large
- Bacon slices, half cup
- Cooked rice, as required

Instructions:
1. Add all the ingredients of the curry into a wok.
2. Cook your bacon strips and chop them.
3. Add the chicken broth and sauces into the mixture.
4. Cook your dish for ten minutes.
5. Add the cooked rice into the mixture.
6. Mix the rice well and cook it for five minutes.
7. Add the egg into the wok by pushing the rest of the ingredients to a side.
8. Add the bacon and then mix the rest of the ingredients into it.
9. Cook your dish for five more minutes.
10. Add the cilantro into the dish.
11. Mix your rice and then dish it out.
12. Your dish is ready to be served.

2.3 Wok Breakfast Omelet Recipe

Preparation Time: 30 minutes
Cooking Time: 10 minutes
Serving: 4

Ingredients:

- Crab rolls, five
- Mushrooms, two
- Onions, half cup
- Rice wine, one tablespoon
- Black pepper, to taste
- Salt, to taste
- Starch, a quarter teaspoon
- Kohlrabi, one cup
- Ginger, one slice
- Soy sauce, one tablespoon
- Oil, one tablespoon
- Cilantro, as required

Instructions:
1. Beat the eggs with water, black pepper and salt.
2. Add oil to a wok, and then add the beaten eggs.
3. Sprinkle the vegetables on top.
4. Add the rest of the ingredients on top of your egg mixture.
5. Fold the egg and then cook it on both sides.
6. When the eggs are done, dish them out.
7. Add on top of the eggs the chopped cilantro leaves.
8. Your dish is ready to be served.

2.4 Wok Breakfast Fried Egg Recipe

Preparation Time: 30 minutes
Cooking Time: 10 minutes
Serving: 4

Ingredients:

- Spring onions, four
- Tortilla, as required
- Pepper to taste
- Butter, as required
- Salt to taste
- Baby plum tomatoes, four
- Eggs, four
- Cilantro, half cup

Instructions:
1. Put the butter in a wok.
2. Add the spring onions and chili into the small wok.
3. Cook for a couple of minutes until softened.
4. Whisk the milk and eggs in a bowl.
5. Add the eggs to the wok.
6. Fry the eggs.
7. Add the tomatoes and coriander leaves on top.
8. Once cooked, dish it out.
9. Your dish is ready to be served.

2.5 Wok Tomato and Egg Stir-Fry Recipe

Preparation Time: 30 minutes
Cooking Time: 10 minutes
Serving: 4

Ingredients:

- Sugar, two teaspoon
- Medium tomatoes, four
- Eggs, four
- White pepper, a quarter teaspoon
- Water, half cup
- Scallions, one
- Sesame oil, two teaspoon
- Vegetable oil, three tablespoon

Instructions:
1. Heat the wok and add the oil.
2. Add the eggs and mix them.
3. Remove the scrambled eggs into a dish.
4. Add one more tablespoon of oil to the wok, and add the tomatoes and scallions.
5. Stir-fry for one minute, and then add two teaspoons of sugar, half teaspoon salt, and a quarter cup water.
6. Add the cooked eggs in the mixture.
7. Your dish is ready to be served.

2.6 Wok Scrambled Egg with Salmon Recipe

Preparation Time: 30 minutes
Cooking Time: 10 minutes
Serving: 4

Ingredients:

- Butter, two tablespoon
- Heavy cream, half cup
- Smoked salmon, half pound
- Salt, to taste
- Black pepper, to taste
- Chopped fresh chives, as required
- Eggs, twelve
- Onions, one
- Chopped garlic, one teaspoon

Instructions:
1. In a large wok, add the butter and let it meltdown.
2. Add in the chopped onion.
3. Cook the onion until soft.
4. Add in the garlic.
5. Mix the onions and garlic for two minutes and add in the smoked salmon.
6. Add the eggs and let it cook.
7. Scramble the mixture.
8. Add in the salt and pepper.
9. Add in the heavy cream in the end.
10. When your eggs are done, dish them out.
11. Add the fresh chopped chives on top.
12. Your dish is ready to be served.

2.7 Wok Meat Breakfast Hash Recipe

Preparation Time: 10 minutes
Cooking Time: 30 minutes
Serving: 4

Ingredients:

- Coconut oil, two tablespoon
- Cinnamon, half teaspoon
- Onion, one
- Shredded carrots, one cup
- Bacon, one pound
- Spinach, two cups
- Dried thyme, half teaspoon
- Powdered ginger, half teaspoon
- Powdered garlic, half teaspoon
- Zucchini, one cup
- Chicken meat, one pound
- Turmeric, half teaspoon
- Butter nut squash, one cup
- Sea salt, to taste

Instructions:
1. Heat the coconut oil in a wok.
2. Add the ground bacon.
3. Once cooked, add in the powdered spices.
4. Remove it from the wok and set it aside.
5. Add in the butternut squash, carrots, zucchini, and chicken.
6. Once they turn soft, add in the spinach as well.
7. Add the spices and cook it for five to ten minutes or until the spinach is wilted.
8. Add in the cooked bacon.

9. Mix your dish well and cook for five minutes.
10. Your dish is ready to be served.

2.8 Wok Shashuka Recipe

Preparation Time: 30 minutes
Cooking Time: 15 minutes
Serving: 3

Ingredients:

- Chopped fresh chives, as required
- Eggs, twelve
- Onions, one
- Chopped garlic, one teaspoon
- Butter, two tablespoon
- Chopped tomatoes, half cup
- Salt, to taste
- Black pepper, to taste

Instructions:
1. In a large wok, add the butter and let it meltdown.
2. Add in the chopped onion.
3. Cook the onion until soft.
4. Add in the garlic.
5. Mix the onions and garlic for two minutes and add in the tomatoes.
6. Add the eggs and do not mix.
7. Add in the salt and pepper.
8. Cover your wok.
9. When the eggs are done, dish them out.
10. Add the fresh chopped chives on top.
11. Your dish is ready to be served.

2.9 Wok Cinnamon Omelet Recipe

Preparation Time: 30 minutes
Cooking Time: 10 minutes
Serving: 4

Ingredients:

- Bean sprouts, one cup
- Fresh coriander leaves, half cup
- Lime juice, one tablespoon
- Cinnamon powder, half teaspoon
- Sliced red chili, one long
- Green beans, one cup
- Vegetable oil, one and a half tablespoon
- Sliced mushrooms, one cup
- Eggs, eight
- Sliced red capsicum, one large
- Chopped tomatoes, two medium sized

Instructions:
1. Beat the eggs, quarter cup water, cinnamon powder, lime juice and a large portion of the chili in an enormous container.
2. Heat two teaspoons of oil in a medium non-stick skillet over medium-high warmth.
3. Cook capsicum and mushrooms, mix, for five minutes or until brilliant and delicate.
4. Add the tomatoes.
5. Cook, mixing, for two minutes or until marginally softened.

6. Boil your green beans in water and then drain them.
7. Combine the mushroom blend, sprouts and beans in a bowl.
8. Warm one teaspoon of remaining oil in skillet over medium-high stove.
9. Pour quarter of the egg mixture into a dish.
10. Cook for thirty seconds or until just set.
11. Slide the omelet onto a plate.
12. Cover the egg to keep it warm.
13. Garnish by sprinkling with coriander and chili.
14. Your dish is ready to be served.

2.10 Wok Crispy Breakfast Rice Recipe

Preparation Time: 30 minutes
Cooking Time: 10 minutes
Serving: 4

Ingredients:

- Red chilies, two
- Sliced green onions, half cup
- White peppercorns, one teaspoon
- Cilantro, one cup
- Fresh ginger, one teaspoon
- Fish sauce, one tablespoon
- Soy sauce, one tablespoon
- Chinese 5 spice, half teaspoon
- Chili garlic sauce, two tablespoon
- Fresh cilantro leaves, half cup
- Fresh basil leaves, a quarter cup
- Vegetable broth, one can

- Minced lemon grass, one teaspoon
- Tofu, one cup
- Cooked rice, as required

Instructions:
1. Add all the ingredients of the curry into a wok.
2. Add the chicken broth and sauces into the mixture.
3. Cook your dish for ten minutes.
4. Add the cooked rice into the mixture.
5. Mix the rice well and cook it for five minutes.
6. Add the tofu into the wok by pushing the rest of the ingredients to a side.
7. Cook your tofu until it turns crunchy and crispy.
8. Cook your dish for five more minutes.
9. Add the cilantro into the dish.
10. Mix your rice and then dish it out.
11. Your dish is ready to be served.

2.11 Wok Spicy Omelet Recipe

Preparation Time: 30 minutes
Cooking Time: 10 minutes
Serving: 4

Ingredients:

- Red chili paste, two tablespoon
- Mushrooms, two
- Eggs, eight
- Onions, half cup
- Rice wine, one tablespoon
- Black pepper, to taste
- Salt, to taste

- Green chilies, a quarter teaspoon
- Ginger, one slice
- Soy sauce, one tablespoon
- Oil, one tablespoon
- Cilantro, as required

Instructions:
1. Beat the eggs with the red wine, black pepper and salt.
2. Add oil to a wok, and then add the beaten eggs.
3. Sprinkle the vegetables on top.
4. Add the rest of the ingredients on top of your egg mixture.
5. Fold the eggs and then cook it on both sides.
6. When the eggs are done, dish them out.
7. Add on top of the eggs the chopped cilantro leaves.
8. Your dish is ready to be served

2.12 Wok Southwest Tofu Scramble Recipe

Preparation Time: 30 minutes
Cooking Time: 10 minutes
Serving: 4

Ingredients:

- Butter, two tablespoon
- Coconut cream, half cup
- Chopped tofu, half pound
- Salt, to taste
- Southwest chili sauce, two tablespoon

- Black pepper, to taste
- Chopped fresh chives, as required
- Eggs, twelve
- Onions, one
- Chopped garlic, one teaspoon

Instructions:
1. In a large wok, add the butter and let it meltdown.
2. Add in the chopped onion.
3. Cook the onion until soft.
4. Add in the garlic.
5. Mix the onions and garlic for two minutes and add in the tofu pieces.
6. Add the eggs and let it cook.
7. Scramble the mixture.
8. Add in the salt and pepper.
9. Add in the coconut cream in the end.
10. When the eggs are done, dish them out.
11. Add the fresh chopped chives on top.
12. Your dish is ready to be served.

Chapter 3: The World of Traditional Wok Lunch Recipes

Following are some classic traditional wok lunch recipes that are rich in healthy nutrients and you can easily make them with the detailed instructions list in each recipe:

3.1 Wok Chicken Stir-Fry Recipe

Preparation Time: 10 minutes
Cooking Time: 20 minutes
Serving: 4

Ingredients:

- Fish sauce, two tablespoon
- Soy sauce, half cup
- Chicken pieces, three cups
- Tomatoes, two
- Cilantro, half cup
- Salt and pepper, to taste
- Minced ginger, half tablespoon
- Vegetable oil, two tablespoon
- Red chili peppers, three
- Toasted nuts, half cup
- Onion, one
- Scallions, half cup
- Minced garlic, one teaspoon

Instructions:
1. In a large wok, add the shallots and oil.

2. Cook your shallots and then add the ginger and garlic.
3. Cook your ginger and garlic and then add in the chicken pieces.
4. Stir fry your chicken pieces well.
5. Add all the spices and the rest of the ingredients into your dish except the toasted nuts.
6. When your chicken is cooked then add the toasted nuts.
7. Cook your dish for five minutes.
8. Garnish your dish with cilantro.
9. Your dish is ready to be served.

3.2 Wok Seared Chicken and Vegetables Recipe

Preparation Time: 30 minutes
Cooking Time: 10 minutes
Serving: 4

Ingredients:

- Coconut cream, one cup
- Chicken stock, two cups
- Minced garlic, one teaspoon
- Minced ginger, one teaspoon
- Brown sugar, two tablespoon
- Shallot, one
- Kaffir lime leaves, four
- Lime wedges
- Lemon grass, two sticks
- Fish sauce, two tablespoon
- Mix vegetables, one cup
- Coconut milk, one cup

- Cilantro, a quarter cup
- Chicken pieces, half pound
- Olive oil, one tablespoon

Instructions:
1. Take a large sauce wok.
2. Add the shallots and olive oil.
3. Cook your shallots and then add the chicken pieces.
4. When the chicken pieces are half cooked then add the chicken stock, minced garlic and ginger.
5. Add the brown sugar and coconut milk.
6. Cook your ingredients until it starts boiling.
7. Add in the mixed vegetables, lemon grass and rest of the ingredients into your dish.
8. Cook your ingredients for ten minutes.
9. Add the coconut cream in the end and mix it for five minutes.
10. Garnish it with cilantro leaves.
11. Your dish is ready to be served.

3.3 Wok Seared Scallops with Tangerine Sauce Recipe

Preparation Time: 30 minutes
Cooking Time: 10 minutes
Serving: 4

Ingredients:

- Hot and sour sauce, one cup
- Vegetable stock, two cups
- Minced garlic, one teaspoon

- Minced ginger, one teaspoon
- Chinese 5 spice, two tablespoon
- Shallot, one
- Kaffir lime leaves, four
- Lime wedges
- Lemon grass, two sticks
- Fish sauce, two tablespoon
- Mix vegetables, one cup
- Cilantro, a quarter cup
- Scallops pieces, half pound
- Tangerine sauce, one cup
- Olive oil, one tablespoon

Instructions:
1. Take a large sauce wok.
2. Add the shallots and olive oil.
3. Cook your shallots and then add the scallop pieces.
4. When the scallop pieces are half cooked then add the vegetable stock, minced garlic and ginger.
5. Add the Chinese 5 spice and the rest of the spices.
6. Cook your ingredients until they start boiling.
7. Add in the mixed vegetables, lemon grass and rest of the ingredients into your dish.
8. Cook your ingredients for ten minutes.
9. Add the tangerine sauce in the end and mix it for five minutes.
10. Garnish it with cilantro leaves.
11. Your dish is ready to be served.

3.4 Wok Stir Cod with Stir-Fried Mushrooms Recipe

Preparation Time: 30 minutes
Cooking Time: 30 minutes
Serving: 4

Ingredients:

- Powdered cumin, one tablespoon
- Salt, to taste
- Black pepper, to taste
- Turmeric powder, one teaspoon
- Onion, one cup
- Vegetable broth, one cup
- Smoked paprika, half teaspoon
- Dijon mustard, half cup
- Cod pieces, one pound
- Minced garlic, two tablespoon
- Minced ginger, two tablespoon
- Cilantro, half cup
- Olive oil, two tablespoon
- Chopped tomatoes, one cup
- Paprika red sauce, one cup
- Chinese red sour and spicy sauce, one cup
- Mushrooms, two cups

Instructions:
1. Take a wok.
2. Add in the oil and onions.
3. Cook the onions until they become soft and fragrant.
4. Add in the chopped garlic and ginger.

5. Cook the mixture and add the tomatoes into it.
6. Add the spices and the Chinese red sour and spicy sauce.
7. When the tomatoes are done, add the pork pieces into it.
8. Mix the codpieces so that the tomatoes and spices are coated all over the cod pieces.
9. Add in the Dijon mustard.
10. Mix the ingredients carefully.
11. Add the mushrooms and cook your dish.
12. Cook the cod for fifteen minutes.
13. When your cod is done, dish it out.
14. Your dish is ready to be served.

3.5 Wok Beef Stir-Fry Recipe

Preparation Time: 10 minutes
Cooking Time: 20 minutes
Serving: 4

Ingredients:

- Fish sauce, two tablespoon
- Soy sauce, half cup
- Beef pieces, three cups
- Tomatoes, two
- Cilantro, half cup
- Salt and pepper, to taste
- Minced ginger, half tablespoon
- Vegetable oil, two tablespoon
- Thai chili peppers, three
- Toasted nuts, half cup
- Onion, one
- Scallions, half cup

- Minced garlic, one teaspoon

Instructions:
1. In a large wok, add the shallots and oil.
2. Cook your shallots and then add the ginger and garlic.
3. Cook your ginger and garlic and then add in the beef pieces.
4. Stir fry your beef pieces well.
5. Add all the spices and the rest of the ingredients into your dish except the toasted nuts.
6. When your beef is cooked then add the toasted nuts.
7. Cook your dish for five minutes.
8. Garnish your dish with cilantro.
9. Your dish is ready to be served.

3.6 Wok Kung Pao Chicken Recipe

Preparation Time: 10 minutes
Cooking Time: 20 minutes
Serving: 4

Ingredients:

- Garlic, one tablespoon
- Peanuts, half cup
- Sesame oil, two teaspoon
- Sichuan pepper, one tablespoon
- Red bell pepper, one
- Green bell pepper, one
- Dried chilies, eight
- Green onions, half cup

- Soy sauce, two tablespoon
- Sugar, two tablespoon
- Chicken one pound
- Baking soda, one teaspoon
- Cornstarch, one teaspoon
- Chicken stock, half cup
- Hoisin sauce, one teaspoon
- Chinese black vinegar, two tablespoon

Instructions:
1. Combine all ingredients for the chicken in a small bowl.
2. Let it rest for ten minutes approximately.
3. Whisk sauce ingredients together until sugar dissolves.
4. Add two tablespoons of cooking oil, allow to heat up, and then add marinated chicken.
5. Fry chicken for approximately four minutes while mixing, until edges are browned.
6. Stir in garlic, ginger, chili diced peppers and Sichuan peppercorns and let it cook for one minute.
7. Give the prepared sauce a mix, then pour it into the wok and bring it to a boil while stirring.
8. Once it begins to thicken slightly, add chicken back into the wok.
9. Mix all of the ingredients through the sauce until the chicken is evenly coated and sauce has thickened.
10. Stir in green onions, peanuts and sesame oil.
11. Toss well and continue to cook for a further two minutes.
12. Your dish is ready to be served.

3.7 Wok Ginger Sesame Tofu Recipe

Preparation Time: 30 minutes
Cooking Time: 10 minutes
Serving: 4

Ingredients:

- Sesame seeds, one cup
- Jalapeno, one large
- Sliced green onions, half cup
- Tofu cubes, two cups
- White peppercorns, one teaspoon
- Cilantro, one cup
- Fresh ginger, one teaspoon
- Fish sauce, one tablespoon
- Soy sauce, one tablespoon
- Chinese 5 spice, half teaspoon
- Chili garlic sauce, two tablespoon
- Fresh cilantro leaves, half cup
- Fresh basil leaves, a quarter cup
- Vegetable broth, one can
- Crushed lemon grass, one teaspoon

Instructions:
1. Add all the ingredients of the sauce into a wok.
2. Add the vegetable broth and sauces into the mixture.
3. Cook your dish for ten minutes.
4. Add the tofu pieces into the mixture once the sauce is ready.

5. Mix the ingredients well and cook it for five minutes.
6. Add the basil leaves and then mix the rest of the ingredients into it.
7. Cook your dish for five more minutes.
8. Add the sesame seeds and cilantro into the dish.
9. Your dish is ready to be served.

3.8 Wok Teriyaki Tofu Rice Recipe

Preparation Time: 30 minutes
Cooking Time: 10 minutes
Serving: 4

Ingredients:

- Chives, one cup
- Vegetable stock, two cups
- Minced garlic, one teaspoon
- Minced ginger, one teaspoon
- Chinese 5 spice, two tablespoon
- Red onion, one
- Kaffir lime leaves, four
- Lime wedges
- Lemon grass, two sticks
- Fish sauce, two tablespoon
- Mix vegetables, one cup
- Cilantro, a quarter cup
- Cooked rice, two cups
- Tofu pieces, half pound
- Teriyaki sauce, one cup
- Olive oil, one tablespoon

Instructions:
1. Take a large sauce wok.
2. Add the shallots and olive oil.
3. Cook your shallots and then add the tofu pieces.
4. When the tofu pieces are half cooked then add the vegetable stock, minced garlic and ginger.
5. Add the Chinese 5 spice and the rest of the spices.
6. Cook your ingredients until they start boiling.
7. Add in the mixed vegetables, lemon grass and rest of the ingredients into your dish.
8. Cook your ingredients for ten minutes.
9. Add the teriyaki sauce and cooked rice in the end and mix it for five minutes.
10. Garnish it with cilantro leaves.
11. Your dish is ready to be served.

3.9 Wok Creamy Tomato Pasta Recipe

Preparation Time: 30 minutes
Cooking Time: 15 minutes
Serving: 4

Ingredients:

- Minced ginger, two tablespoon
- Cilantro, half cup
- Coconut milk, one cup
- Olive oil, two tablespoon

- Cherry tomatoes, one cup
- Pasta, one pack
- Vegetable broth, one cup
- Turmeric powder, one teaspoon
- Onion, one cup
- Coconut cream, one cup
- Smoked paprika, half teaspoon
- Water, one cup
- Minced garlic, two tablespoon

Instructions:
1. Take a wok.
2. Add in the oil and onions.
3. Cook the onions until they become soft and fragrant.
4. Add in the chopped garlic and ginger.
5. Cook the mixture and add the coconut cream and coconut milk into it.
6. Add the spices.
7. Add in the broth.
8. Mix the ingredients carefully and cover your wok.
9. Boil your pasta according to the instructions on the package.
10. When your coconut milk is cooked, add in the cherry tomatoes.
11. Mix the pasta into the mixture.
12. Add cilantro on top.
13. Your dish is ready to be served.

3.10 Wok Kung Pao Shrimp Recipe

Preparation Time: 10 minutes
Cooking Time: 20 minutes
Serving: 4

Ingredients:

- Garlic, one tablespoon
- Peanuts, half cup
- Sesame oil, two teaspoon
- Sichuan pepper, one tablespoon
- Red bell pepper, one
- Green bell pepper, one
- Dried chilies, eight
- Green onions, half cup
- Soy sauce, two tablespoon
- Sugar, two tablespoon
- Shrimps, one pound
- Baking soda, one teaspoon
- Cornstarch, one teaspoon
- Fish stock, half cup
- Hoisin sauce, one teaspoon
- Chinese black vinegar, two tablespoon

Instructions:
1. Combine all ingredients for the shrimps in a small bowl.
2. Let it rest for ten minutes approximately.
3. Whisk sauce ingredients together until sugar dissolves.
4. Add two tablespoons of cooking oil, allow to heat up, and then add marinated shrimp.

5. Fry shrimp for approximately four minutes while mixing, until edges are browned.
6. Stir in garlic, ginger, chili diced peppers and Sichuan peppercorns and let it cook for one minute.
7. Give the prepared sauce a mix, then pour it into the wok and bring it to a boil while stirring.
8. Once it begins to thicken slightly, add shrimps back into the wok.
9. Mix all of the ingredients through the sauce until the shrimps are evenly coated and sauce has thickened.
10. Stir in green onions, peanuts and sesame oil.
11. Toss well and continue to cook for a further two minutes.
12. Your dish is ready to be served.

3.11 Wok Chicken Sausage and Vegetable Curry Recipe

Preparation Time: 30 minutes
Cooking Time: 10 minutes
Serving: 4

Ingredients:

- Galangal, one can
- Chicken stock, two cups
- Minced garlic, one teaspoon
- Palm sugar, two tablespoon
- Shallot, one
- Kaffir lime leaves, four
- Lime wedges

- Mixed vegetables, one cup
- Lemon grass, two sticks
- Fish sauce, two tablespoon
- Thai red curry paste, two tablespoon
- Coconut milk, one cup
- Cilantro, a quarter cup
- Chicken sausages, half pound
- Olive oil, one tablespoon

Instructions:
1. Take a large sauce wok.
2. Add the shallots and olive oil.
3. Cook your shallots and then add the chicken sausage.
4. When the sausages are half cooked, add the galangal, red curry paste, chicken stock, and minced garlic.
5. Add the vegetables and coconut milk.
6. Cook your ingredients until they start boiling.
7. Add in the lemon grass and rest of the ingredients into the curry.
8. Cook your ingredients for ten minutes.
9. When your curry is cooked, dish it out.
10. Garnish it with cilantro leaves.
11. Your dish is ready to be served.

3.12 Wok Crispy Tofu and Vegetable Stir-Fry Recipe

Preparation Time: 30 minutes
Cooking Time: 10 minutes
Serving: 4

Ingredients:

- Mixed vegetables, one cup
- Vegetable stock, two cups
- Minced garlic, one teaspoon
- Palm sugar, two tablespoon
- Shallot, one
- Kaffir lime leaves, four
- Lime wedges
- Lemon grass, two sticks
- Fish sauce, two tablespoon
- Thai red curry paste, two tablespoon
- Coconut milk, one cup
- Cilantro, a quarter cup
- Tofu cubes, half pound
- Sesame oil, one tablespoon
- Olive oil, one tablespoon
-

Instructions:
1. Take a large sauce wok.
2. Add the shallots and olive oil.
3. Cook your shallots and then add the mixed vegetables.
4. When the mixed vegetables are half cooked, add the galangal, red curry paste, chicken stock, and minced garlic.
5. Add the palm sugar and coconut milk.
6. Cook your ingredients until they start boiling.
7. Add in the lemon grass and rest of the ingredients into the dish.
8. In a separate wok, add the sesame oil and tofu cubes.
9. Cook your tofu cubes until they turn crispy.

10. Add the tofu cubes into your dish.
11. Cook your ingredients for ten minutes.
12. When your dish is cooked, dish it out.
13. Garnish it with cilantro leaves.
14. Your dish is ready to be served.

3.13 Wok Shredded Pork with Crispy Tofu Recipe

Preparation Time: 30 minutes
Cooking Time: 10 minutes
Serving: 4

Ingredients:

- Mixed vegetables, one cup
- Vegetable stock, two cups
- Shaoxing wine, half cup
- Shredded pork, half pound
- Minced garlic, one teaspoon
- Brown sugar, two tablespoon
- Shallot, one
- Kaffir lime leaves, four
- Lime wedges
- Lemon grass, two sticks
- Fish sauce, two tablespoon
- Thai red curry paste, two tablespoon
- Coconut milk, one cup
- Cilantro, a quarter cup
- Tofu cubes, half pound
- Sesame oil, one tablespoon
- Olive oil, one tablespoon

Instructions:
1. Take a large sauce wok.
2. Add the shallots and olive oil.
3. Cook your shallots and then add the mixed vegetables.
4. When the mixed vegetables are half cooked, add the shredded pork, red curry paste, chicken stock, and minced garlic.
5. Add the curry leaves and coconut milk.
6. Cook your ingredients until they start boiling.
7. Add in the Shaoxing wine and rest of the ingredients into the dish.
8. In a separate wok, add the sesame oil and tofu cubes.
9. Cook your tofu cubes until they turn crispy.
10. Add the tofu cubes into your dish.
11. Cook your ingredients for ten minutes.
12. When your dish is cooked, dish it out.
13. Garnish it with cilantro leaves.
14. Your dish is ready to be served.

3.14 Wok Sweet and Sour Chicken Recipe

Preparation Time: 30 minutes
Cooking Time: 10 minutes
Serving: 4

Ingredients:

- Chives, one cup
- Chicken stock, two cups
- Minced garlic, one teaspoon
- Minced ginger, one teaspoon
- Chinese 5 spice, two tablespoon

- Red onion, one
- Kaffir lime leaves, four
- Lime wedges
- Lemon grass, two sticks
- Fish sauce, two tablespoon
- Mix vegetables, one cup
- Cilantro, a quarter cup
- Chicken pieces, half pound
- Sweet and sour sauce, one cup
- Olive oil, one tablespoon

Instructions:
1. Take a large sauce wok.
2. Add the shallots and olive oil.
3. Cook your shallots and then add the chicken pieces.
4. When the chicken pieces are half cooked then add the chicken stock, minced garlic and ginger.
5. Add the Chinese 5 spice and the rest of the spices.
6. Cook your ingredients until they start boiling.
7. Add in the mixed vegetables, lemon grass and rest of the ingredients into your dish.
8. Cook your ingredients for ten minutes.
9. Add the sweet and sour sauce and chives in the end and mix it for five minutes.
10. Garnish it with cilantro leaves.
11. Your dish is ready to be served.

3.15 Wok Mongolian Beef and Broccoli Recipe

Preparation Time: 10 minutes
Cooking Time: 20 minutes
Serving: 4

Ingredients:

- Fish sauce, two tablespoon
- Soy sauce, half cup
- Mongolian spice mix, two tablespoon
- Beef pieces, three cups
- Tomatoes, two
- Broccoli florets, two cups
- Cilantro, half cup
- Salt and pepper, to taste
- Minced ginger, half tablespoon
- Vegetable oil, two tablespoon
- Red chili peppers, three
- Toasted nuts, half cup
- Onion, one
- Scallions, half cup
- Minced garlic, one teaspoon

Instructions:
1. In a large wok, add the shallots and oil.
2. Cook your shallots and then add the ginger and garlic.
3. Cook your ginger and garlic and then add in the beef pieces.
4. Stir fry your beef pieces well.

5. Add the Mongolian spice mix and the rest of the ingredients into your dish except the toasted nuts.
6. When your beef is cooked then add the broccoli florets.
7. Cook your dish for five minutes.
8. Add the toasted nuts two minutes before switching off your stove.
9. Garnish your dish with cilantro.
10. Your dish is ready to be served.

3.16 Wok Coconut Curry Noodle Soup Recipe

Preparation Time: 30 minutes
Cooking Time: 10 minutes
Serving: 4

Ingredients:

- Water, two cups
- Rice noodles, one pack
- Galangal, one can
- Vegetable stock, two cups
- Minced garlic, one teaspoon
- Minced ginger, one teaspoon
- Chopped onion, half cup
- Minced ginger, half tablespoon
- Lemon grass, two sticks
- Fish sauce, two tablespoon
- Shredded coconut, one cup
- Coconut milk, one cup
- Cilantro, a quarter cup

- Olive oil, one tablespoon

Instructions:
1. Take a large sauce wok.
2. Add the chopped onion and olive oil.
3. Cook your chopped onion.
4. When the onions are cooked then add the galangal, vegetable stock, minced garlic and ginger.
5. Add the coconut milk.
6. Cook your ingredients until they start boiling.
7. Add in the shredded coconut, lemon grass and rest of the ingredients into your curry.
8. Now add the water and noodles into the dish.
9. Cook your ingredients for ten minutes.
10. Garnish it with cilantro leaves.
11. Your dish is ready to be served.

3.17 Wok Crispy Tofu in Ginger and Garlic Sauce Recipe

Preparation Time: 30 minutes
Cooking Time: 10 minutes
Serving: 4

Ingredients:

- Mixed vegetables, one cup
- Vegetable stock, two cups
- Minced garlic, one teaspoon
- Garlic and ginger sauce, one cup
- Shallot, one

- Kaffir lime leaves, four
- Lime wedges
- Lemon grass, two sticks
- Fish sauce, two tablespoon
- Thai red curry paste, two tablespoon
- Coconut milk, one cup
- Cilantro, a quarter cup
- Tofu cubes, half pound
- Sesame oil, one tablespoon
- Olive oil, one tablespoon

Instructions:
1. Take a large sauce wok.
2. Add the shallots and olive oil.
3. Cook your shallots and then add the mixed vegetables.
4. Add the ginger and garlic sauce and coconut milk.
5. Cook your ingredients until they start boiling.
6. Add in the lemon grass and rest of the ingredients into the dish.
7. In a separate wok, add the sesame oil and tofu cubes.
8. Cook your tofu cubes until they turn crispy.
9. Add the tofu cubes into your dish.
10. Cook your ingredients for ten minutes.
11. When your dish is cooked, dish it out.
12. Garnish it with cilantro leaves.
13. Your dish is ready to be served.

3.18 Wok Beef and Mushroom Stew Recipe

Preparation Time: 30 minutes
Cooking Time: 10 minutes

Serving: 4

Ingredients:

- Red sauce, half cup
- Beef stock, two cups
- Minced garlic, one teaspoon
- Brown sugar, two tablespoon
- Shallot, one
- Ginger pieces, a quarter cup
- Beef pieces, half pound
- Kaffir lime leaves, four
- Lemon grass, two sticks
- Fish sauce, two tablespoon
- Wild mushroom, one cup
- Coconut milk, one cup
- Cilantro, a quarter cup
- Beef chunks, half pound
- Olive oil, one tablespoon

Instructions:
1. Take a large sauce wok.
2. Add the shallots and olive oil.
3. Cook your shallots and then add the beef chunks.
4. When the beef chunks are cooked then add the red sauce, beef stock, and minced garlic.
5. Add the ginger pieces and coconut milk.
6. Cook your ingredients until they start boiling.
7. Add in the mushrooms and rest of the ingredients into your stew.
8. Cook your ingredients for ten minutes.
9. When your mushrooms are cooked, dish out your stew.

10. Garnish it with cilantro leaves.
11. Your dish is ready to be served.

Chapter 4: The World of Traditional Wok Dinner Recipes

Following are some classic traditional wok dinner recipes that are rich in healthy nutrients and you can easily make them with the detailed instructions list in each recipe:

4.1 Wok Black Pepper Chicken Recipe

Preparation Time: 30 minutes
Cooking Time: 20 minutes
Serving: 4

Ingredients:

- Minced garlic, two tablespoon
- Minced ginger, two tablespoon
- Cilantro, half cup
- Olive oil, two tablespoon
- Chopped tomatoes, one cup
- Powdered cumin, one tablespoon
- Salt, to taste
- Black pepper, two tablespoon
- Turmeric powder, one teaspoon
- Onion, one cup
- Vegetable broth, one cup
- Smoked paprika, half teaspoon
- Water, half cup
- Chicken breast, one pound

Instructions:
1. Take a wok.
2. Add in the oil and onions.
3. Cook the onions until they become soft and fragrant.
4. Add in the chopped garlic and ginger.
5. Cook the mixture and add the tomatoes into it.
6. Add the spices.
7. When the tomatoes are done, add the chicken into it.
8. Mix the chicken so that the tomatoes and spices are coated all over the chicken.
9. Cook for five minutes.
10. Add in the water.
11. Mix the ingredients carefully and cover your wok.
12. When your chicken is done, add in the cilantro.
13. Mix your chicken and let it cook for an additional five minutes.
14. Your dish is ready to be served.

4.2 Wok Thai Chili Basil Chicken Recipe

Preparation Time: 30 minutes
Cooking Time: 10 minutes
Serving: 4

Ingredients:

- Red chilies, two
- Jalapeno, one large
- Sliced green onions, half cup
- Chicken pieces, two cups

- White peppercorns, one teaspoon
- Cilantro, one cup
- Fresh ginger, one teaspoon
- Fish sauce, one tablespoon
- Soy sauce, one tablespoon
- Chinese 5 spice, half teaspoon
- Chili garlic sauce, two tablespoon
- Fresh cilantro leaves, half cup
- Fresh basil leaves, a quarter cup
- Chicken broth, one can
- Minced lemon grass, one teaspoon

Instructions:
1. Add all the ingredients of the sauce into a wok.
2. Add the chicken broth and sauces into the mixture.
3. Cook your dish for ten minutes.
4. Add the chicken pieces and tofu pieces into the mixture once the sauce is ready.
5. Mix the ingredients well and cook it for five minutes.
6. Add the basil leaves and chili.
7. Mix the rest of the ingredients into it.
8. Cook your dish for five more minutes.
9. Add the cilantro into the dish.
10. Your dish is ready to be served.

4.3 Wok Spicy Chicken with Peanuts Recipe

Preparation Time: 30 minutes

Cooking Time: 10 minutes
Serving: 4

Ingredients:

- Red chili paste, one tablespoon
- Mixed vegetables, two cups
- Minced garlic, one teaspoon
- Minced ginger, one teaspoon
- Chopped onion, half cup
- Chicken pieces, half pound
- Peanuts, one cup
- Minced ginger, half tablespoon
- Lemon grass, two sticks
- Fish sauce, two tablespoon
- Spicy peanut sauce, one cup
- Coconut milk, one cup
- Cilantro, a quarter cup
- Olive oil, one tablespoon

Instructions:
1. Take a large sauce wok.
2. Add the chopped onion and olive oil.
3. Cook your chopped onion and then add the chicken and vegetables.
4. Add the coconut milk.
5. Cook your ingredients until they start boiling.
6. Add in the peanuts, spicy peanut sauce and the rest of the ingredients.
7. Cook your ingredients for ten minutes.
8. Garnish it with cilantro leaves.
9. Your dish is ready to be served.

4.4 Wok Beef with Broccoli and Oyster Sauce Recipe

Preparation Time: 10 minutes
Cooking Time: 20 minutes
Serving: 4

Ingredients:

- Oyster sauce, half cup
- Fish sauce, two tablespoon
- Soy sauce, half cup
- Chinese spice mix, two tablespoon
- Beef pieces, three cups
- Tomatoes, two
- Broccoli florets, two cups
- Cilantro, half cup
- Salt and pepper, to taste
- Minced ginger, half tablespoon
- Vegetable oil, two tablespoon
- Red chili peppers, three
- Toasted nuts, half cup
- Onion, one
- Scallions, half cup
- Minced garlic, one teaspoon

Instructions:
1. In a large wok, add the shallots and oil.
2. Cook your shallots and then add the ginger and garlic.
3. Cook your ginger and garlic and then add in the beef pieces.
4. Stir fry your beef pieces well.

5. Add the spices and the rest of the ingredients into your dish except the toasted nuts.
6. When your beef is cooked then add the broccoli florets.
7. Cook your dish for five minutes.
8. Add the oyster sauce in the dish.
9. Add the toasted nuts two minutes before switching off your stove.
10. Garnish your dish with cilantro.
11. Your dish is ready to be served.

4.5 Wok Spicy Chicken and Leek Stir-Fry Recipe

Preparation Time: 30 minutes
Cooking Time: 10 minutes
Serving: 4

Ingredients:

- Red chili paste, one tablespoon
- Mixed vegetables, two cups
- Minced garlic, one teaspoon
- Minced ginger, one teaspoon
- Chopped onion, half cup
- Chicken pieces, half pound
- Minced ginger, half tablespoon
- Lemon grass, two sticks
- Fish sauce, two tablespoon
- Chopped leeks, one cup
- Coconut milk, one cup
- Cilantro, a quarter cup
- Olive oil, one tablespoon

Instructions:
1. Take a large sauce wok.
2. Add the chopped onion and olive oil.
3. Cook your chopped onion and then add the chicken.
4. Add the coconut milk.
5. Cook your ingredients until they start boiling.
6. Add in the chopped leeks, red chili paste and the rest of the ingredients.
7. Cook your ingredients for ten minutes.
8. Garnish it with cilantro leaves.
9. Your dish is ready to be served.

4.6 Wok Almond and Vegetable Stir-Fry Recipe

Preparation Time: 10 minutes
Cooking Time: 20 minutes
Serving: 4

Ingredients:

- Fish sauce, two tablespoon
- Soy sauce, half cup
- Mixed vegetables, three cups
- Tomatoes, two
- Cilantro, half cup
- Salt and pepper, to taste
- Minced ginger, half tablespoon
- Vegetable oil, two tablespoon
- Red chili peppers, three
- Toasted almonds, half cup
- Onion, one

- Scallions, half cup
- Minced garlic, one teaspoon

Instructions:
1. In a large wok, add the shallots and oil.
2. Cook your shallots and then add the ginger and garlic.
3. Cook your ginger and garlic and then add in the mixed vegetables.
4. Stir fry your vegetables.
5. Add all the spices and the rest of the ingredients into your dish except the toasted almonds.
6. When your vegetables are cooked, add the toasted almonds.
7. Cook your dish for five minutes.
8. Garnish your dish with cilantro.
9. Your dish is ready to be served.

4.7 Wok Sweet and Sour Beef Recipe

Preparation Time: 30 minutes
Cooking Time: 10 minutes
Serving: 4

Ingredients:

- Chives, one cup
- Beef stock, two cups
- Minced garlic, one teaspoon
- Minced ginger, one teaspoon
- Chinese 5 spice, two tablespoon
- Red onion, one
- Kaffir lime leaves, four

- Lime wedges
- Lemon grass, two sticks
- Fish sauce, two tablespoon
- Mix vegetables, one cup
- Cilantro, a quarter cup
- Beef pieces, half pound
- Sweet and sour sauce, one cup
- Olive oil, one tablespoon

Instructions:
1. Take a large sauce wok.
2. Add the shallots and olive oil.
3. Cook your shallots and then add the beef chunks.
4. When the beef chunks are half cooked then add the beef stock, minced garlic and ginger.
5. Add the Chinese 5 spice and the rest of the spices.
6. Cook your ingredients until they start boiling.
7. Add in the mixed vegetables, lemon grass and rest of the ingredients into your dish.
8. Cook your ingredients for ten minutes.
9. Add the sweet and sour sauce and chives in the end and mix it for five minutes.
10. Garnish it with cilantro leaves.
11. Your dish is ready to be served.

4.8 Wok Turkey and Asparagus Stir-Fry Recipe

Preparation Time: 10 minutes
Cooking Time: 20 minutes
Serving: 4

Ingredients:

- Fish sauce, two tablespoon
- Soy sauce, half cup
- Minced turkey meat, three cups
- Tomatoes, two
- Cilantro, half cup
- Salt and pepper, to taste
- Minced ginger, half tablespoon
- Vegetable oil, two tablespoon
- Red chili peppers, three
- Chopped asparagus, one cup
- Onion, one
- Scallions, half cup
- Minced garlic, one teaspoon

Instructions:
1. In a large wok, add the shallots and oil.
2. Cook your shallots and then add the ginger and garlic.
3. Cook the ginger and garlic and then add in the minced turkey meat.
4. Stir fry the turkey meat.

5. Add all the spices and the rest of the ingredients into your dish except the chopped asparagus.
6. When your turkey is cooked then, add the chopped asparagus.
7. Cook your dish for five minutes.
8. Garnish your dish with cilantro.
9. Your dish is ready to be served.

4.9 Wok Coconut and Shrimp Curry Recipe

Preparation Time: 30 minutes
Cooking Time: 20 minutes
Serving: 4

Ingredients:

- Galangal, one can
- Fish stock, two cups
- Minced garlic, one teaspoon
- Minced ginger, one teaspoon
- Chopped onion, half cup
- Minced ginger, half tablespoon
- Lemon grass, two sticks
- Fish sauce, two tablespoon
- Shredded coconut, one cup
- Coconut milk, one cup
- Cilantro, a quarter cup
- Shrimp meat, half pound
- Olive oil, one tablespoon

Instructions:
1. Take a large sauce wok.
2. Add the chopped onion and olive oil.

3. Cook your chopped onion and then add the shrimp meat.
4. When the shrimp meat is half cooked then add the galangal, fish stock, minced garlic and ginger.
5. Add the coconut milk.
6. Cook your ingredients until they start boiling.
7. Add in the shredded coconut, lemon grass and rest of the ingredients into your curry.
8. Cook your ingredients for ten minutes.
9. When your shrimp meat is cooked completely dish out your curry.
10. Garnish it with cilantro leaves.
11. Your dish is ready to be served.

4.10 Wok Mandarin Pork Stir-Fry Recipe

Preparation Time: 10 minutes
Cooking Time: 20 minutes
Serving: 4

Ingredients:

- Mandarin sauce, half cup
- Fish sauce, two tablespoon
- Soy sauce, half cup
- Pork pieces, three cups
- Tomatoes, two
- Cilantro, half cup
- Salt and pepper, to taste
- Minced ginger, half tablespoon
- Vegetable oil, two tablespoon
- Red chili peppers, three
- Toasted nuts, half cup

- Onion, one
- Scallions, half cup
- Minced garlic, one teaspoon

Instructions:
1. In a large wok, add the shallots and oil.
2. Cook your shallots and then add the ginger and garlic.
3. Cook your ginger and garlic and then add in the pork pieces.
4. Stir fry your pork pieces well.
5. Add the mandarin sauce into the dish.
6. Add all the spices and the rest of the ingredients into your dish except the toasted nuts.
7. When your pork is cooked then add the toasted nuts.
8. Cook your dish for five minutes.
9. Garnish your dish with cilantro.
10. Your dish is ready to be served.

4.11 Wok Scallops and Asparagus Stir-Fry Recipe

Preparation Time: 10 minutes
Cooking Time: 20 minutes
Serving: 4

Ingredients:

- Fish sauce, two tablespoon
- Soy sauce, half cup
- Scallops, three cups
- Tomatoes, two

- Cilantro, half cup
- Salt and pepper, to taste
- Minced ginger, half tablespoon
- Vegetable oil, two tablespoon
- Red chili peppers, three
- Chopped asparagus, one cup
- Onion, one
- Scallions, half cup
- Minced garlic, one teaspoon

Instructions:
1. In a large wok, add the shallots and oil.
2. Cook your shallots and then add the ginger and garlic.
3. Cook your ginger and garlic and then add in the scallops.
4. Stir fry your scallops.
5. Add all the spices and the rest of the ingredients into your dish except the chopped asparagus.
6. When your scallops are cooked then, add the chopped asparagus.
7. Cook your dish for five minutes.
8. Garnish your dish with cilantro.
9. Your dish is ready to be served.

4.12 Wok Mexican Steak Stir-Fry Recipe

Preparation Time: 10 minutes
Cooking Time: 20 minutes

Serving: 4

Ingredients:

- Mexican hot sauce, half cup
- Fish sauce, two tablespoon
- Soy sauce, half cup
- Steak pieces, three cups
- Tomatoes, two
- Cilantro, half cup
- Salt and pepper, to taste
- Minced ginger, half tablespoon
- Vegetable oil, two tablespoon
- Red chili peppers, three
- Onion, one
- Scallions, half cup
- Minced garlic, one teaspoon

Instructions:
1. In a large wok, add the shallots and oil.
2. Cook your shallots and then add the ginger and garlic.
3. Cook your ginger and garlic and then add in the steak pieces.
4. Stir fry your steak pieces well.
5. Add all the spices and the rest of the ingredients into your dish except the Mexican hot sauce.
6. When your steak pieces are cooked then add the Mexican hot sauce.
7. Cook your dish for five minutes.
8. Garnish your dish with cilantro.
9. Your dish is ready to be served.

4.13 Wok Orange and Beef Stir-Fry Recipe

Preparation Time: 10 minutes
Cooking Time: 20 minutes
Serving: 4

Ingredients:

- Shredded orange peel, two tablespoon
- Soy sauce, half cup
- Beef meat, one pound
- Tomatoes, two
- Cilantro, half cup
- Salt and pepper, to taste
- Minced ginger, half tablespoon
- Vegetable oil, two tablespoon
- Red chili peppers, three
- Orange juice, one cup
- Onion, one
- Scallions, half cup
- Minced garlic, one teaspoon

Instructions:
1. In a large wok, add the shallots and oil.
2. Cook your shallots and then add the ginger and garlic.
3. Cook your ginger and garlic and then add in the beef meat.
4. Stir fry your beef meat.
5. Add all the spices and the rest of the ingredients into your dish except the orange juice and shredded orange peels.

6. When your beef is cooked, add the orange juice and shredded orange peel.
7. Cook your dish for five minutes.
8. Garnish your dish with cilantro.
9. Your dish is ready to be served.

4.14 Wok Chicken Soba Noodles Recipe

Preparation Time: 30 minutes
Cooking Time: 10 minutes
Serving: 4

Ingredients:

- Mixed vegetables, two cups
- Sliced green onions, half cup
- White peppercorns, one teaspoon
- Cilantro, one cup
- Fresh ginger, one teaspoon
- Fish sauce, one tablespoon
- Soy sauce, one tablespoon
- Chinese 5 spice, half teaspoon
- Chili garlic sauce, two tablespoon
- Fresh cilantro leaves, half cup
- Fresh basil leaves, a quarter cup
- Chicken broth, one cup
- Chicken pieces, half pound
- Soba noodles, as required

Instructions:
1. Add all the ingredients of the sauce into a wok.
2. Add the chicken pieces, vegetables, chicken broth and sauces into the mixture.
3. Cook your dish for ten minutes.

4. Add the soba noodles into the mixture once the sauce is ready.
5. Mix the noodles well and cook it for five minutes.
6. Add the cilantro into the dish.
7. Cook your noodles and then dish it out.
8. Your dish is ready to be served.

4.15 Wok Pineapple Fried Rice Recipe

Preparation Time: 30 minutes
Cooking Time: 10 minutes
Serving: 4

Ingredients:

- Red chilies, two
- Sliced green onions, half cup
- White peppercorns, one teaspoon
- Cilantro, one cup
- Fresh ginger, one teaspoon
- Fish sauce, one tablespoon
- Soy sauce, one tablespoon
- Chinese 5 spice, half teaspoon
- Chili garlic sauce, two tablespoon
- Fresh cilantro leaves, half cup
- Fresh basil leaves, a quarter cup
- Vegetable broth, one can
- Minced lemon grass, one teaspoon
- Pineapple chunks, two cup
- Cooked rice, as required

Instructions:
1. Add all the ingredients of the curry into a wok.
2. Add the vegetable broth and sauces into the mixture.
3. Cook your dish for ten minutes.
4. Add the cooked rice into the mixture.
5. Mix the rice well and cook it for five minutes.
6. Add the pineapple chunks into the wok.
7. Cook your pineapple chunks.
8. Cook your dish for five more minutes.
9. Add the cilantro into the dish.
10. Mix your rice and then dish it out.
11. Your dish is ready to be served.

Chapter 5: The World of Traditional Wok Dessert Recipes

Following are some classic traditional wok dessert recipes that are rich in healthy nutrients and you can easily make them with the detailed instructions list in each recipe:

5.1 Wok Stir-Fried Bananas Foster Recipe

Preparation Time: 10 minutes
Cooking Time: 30 minutes
Serving: 2

Ingredients:

- Vanilla extract, one teaspoon
- Cinnamon powder, a quarter teaspoon
- Unsalted butter six tablespoon
- Dark rum, a quarter cup
- Dark brown sugar, one cup
- Vanilla ice cream, as required
- Peeled firm bananas, four

Instructions:
1. Take a large bowl.
2. Add the brown sugar, butter and cinnamon powder.
3. Beat your butter mixture until the brown sugar melts down.
4. Heat a wok.
5. Add your butter mixture into the wok.
6. Add the peeled firm bananas into the butter.

7. Cook your dark rum and vanilla extract into the wok.
8. When your bananas are cooked properly, dish them out.
9. Add the vanilla ice cream on top of your bananas.
10. Your dish is ready to be served.

5.2 Wok Stir-Fried Apples Shortcake Recipe

Preparation Time: 10 minutes
Cooking Time: 40 minutes
Serving: 2

Ingredients:

- Ground cinnamon, half teaspoon
- Chopped mixed peel, one tablespoon
- Self-rising flour, one cup
- Mixed spice, one teaspoon
- Milk, one tablespoon
- Baking powder, one teaspoon
- Apple slices, three
- Eggs, two
- Butter, half cup
- Brown sugar, one cup
- Orange zest, half cup

Instructions:
1. Take a wok.
2. Add the butter.
3. When it melts down add the apple slices.
4. Cook your apples.
5. Switch off the stove.

6. Add the mixture into a bowl.
7. Add the rest of the ingredients and mix.
8. Add the mixture into a dish.
9. Grease your dish.
10. Add the dish into a wok full of water.
11. Make sure the water is below the level of the dish.
12. Cover the wok.
13. Steam your cake for fifteen to twenty minutes.
14. Your dish is ready to be served.

5.3 Wok Steamed Red Bean Bun Recipe

Preparation Time: 50 minutes
Cooking Time: 30 minutes
Serving: 4

Ingredients:

- Red beans, half pound
- Thin soy sauce, one tablespoon
- Cinnamon powder, half tablespoon
- White sugar, one tablespoon
- Sweet vinegar, one tablespoon
- Brown powder, one tablespoon
- Fresh shallot, half tablespoon
- Milk, one cup
- Vegetable oil, one tablespoon
- All-purpose flour, one cup
- Whole wheat flour, half cup
- Salt, to taste
- Water, to knead
- Yeast, one cup

Instructions:
1. Take a bowl and add the flour into it.
2. Then add the yeast and sugar into it.
3. Add lukewarm water in it.
4. Set aside for half an hour.
5. In another bowl, take the whole wheat flour.
6. Add the yeast dough in it.
7. Then add the salt and some water in it.
8. Then combine the ingredients to form a soft dough.
9. Knead it for ten minutes.
10. Meanwhile, grind the red beans.
11. Mix them with soy sauce, sweet vinegar, sugar and salt.
12. Make round forms of dough with the help of the oil.
13. Then bake your buns for ten minutes.
14. Once the buns are steamed, take them out.
15. You can serve red beans buns.

5.4 Wok Steamed Coconut Bun Recipe

Preparation Time: 50 minutes
Cooking Time: 30 minutes
Serving: 4

Ingredients:

- Sweet coconut, half pound
- Thin soy sauce, one tablespoon
- Cinnamon powder, half tablespoon
- White sugar, one tablespoon
- Sweet vinegar, one tablespoon
- Brown powder, one tablespoon
- Milk, one cup
- Vegetable oil, one tablespoon
- All-purpose flour, one cup
- Whole wheat flour, half cup
- Salt, to taste
- Water, to knead
- Yeast, one cup

Instructions:
1. Take a bowl and add the flour into it.
2. Then add the yeast and sugar into it.
3. Add lukewarm water in it.
4. Set aside for half hour.
5. In another bowl, take the whole wheat flour.
6. Add the yeast dough in it.
7. Then add the salt and some water in it.
8. Then combine the ingredients to form a soft dough.
9. Knead it for ten minutes.
10. Meanwhile, grind the coconut cubes.
11. Mix them with soy sauce, sweet vinegar, sugar and salt.
12. Make round forms of dough with the help of the oil.

13. Then bake your buns for ten minutes.
14. Once the buns are steamed, take them out.
15. You can serve red beans buns.

5.5 Wok Sesame Balls Recipe

Preparation Time: 10 minutes
Cooking Time: 10 minutes
Serving: 4

Ingredients:

- Glutinous rice flour, three cups
- White sesame seeds, a quarter cup
- Vegetable oil, two tablespoon
- Brown sugar, two cups
- Black sesame seeds, a quarter cup
- Sweetened red bean paste, one cup

Instructions:
1. Heat a wok.
2. Add the vegetable oil in the wok.
3. Add the white and black sesame seeds.
4. Cook them for five minutes.
5. Add the glutinous rice flour and brown sugar into the wok.
6. Add the sweetened red bean paste into the mixture.
7. Cook your dish and then dish out.
8. When the mixture turns a little cold, make small round balls from the mixture.
9. Your dish is ready to be served.

5.6 Wok Snow Skin Mooncakes Recipe

Preparation Time: 30 minutes
Cooking Time: 10 minutes
Serving: 4

Ingredients:

- Glutinous rice flour, three cups
- Simple rice flour, one cup
- Wheat starch, a quarter cup
- Vegetable oil, two tablespoon
- Brown sugar, two cups
- Ground cinnamon, half teaspoon
- Whole milk, a quarter cup
- Sweetened red mung bean paste, one cup

Instructions:
1. In a bowl, add all the wet ingredients except the red mung bean paste.
2. Add the dry ingredients into a separate bowl.
3. Add the dry ingredients into the wet ingredients.
4. Take a cupcake mold.
5. Grease your mold and then add the mixture into the mold.
6. Add the mung bean paste into each cupcake.
7. Add the rice mixture on top again to cover the bean paste.
8. Steam your cakes in a wok.
9. Your dish is ready to be served.

5.7 Wok Steamed White Sugar Sponge Cake Recipe

Preparation Time: 10 minutes
Cooking Time: 40 minutes
Serving: 2

Ingredients:

- Self-rising flour, one cup
- Milk, one tablespoon
- Baking powder, one teaspoon
- Eggs, two
- Butter, half cup
- White sugar, one cup

Instructions:
1. Add all the ingredients and mix.
2. Grease your dish.
3. Add the mixture into a dish.
4. Put the dish into a wok full of water.
5. Make sure the water is below the level of the dish.
6. Cover the wok.
7. Steam your cake for fifteen to twenty minutes.
8. Your dish is ready to be served.

5.8 Wok Peach Squares Recipe

Preparation Time: 10 minutes
Cooking Time: 40 minutes
Serving: 2

Ingredients:

- Powdered sugar, one cup
- Sugar, one cup
- Vanilla extract, one teaspoon
- Eggs, two
- Peach slices, one cup
- Salted butter, one cup
- Walnut pieces, one cup
- All-purpose flour, one and a half cup

Instructions:
1. Take a wok.
2. Add the salted butter into the wok.
3. Add the peach slices into the wok.
4. Switch off the stove.
5. In a bowl, add the sugar and eggs.
6. Beat the eggs and powdered sugar.
7. Add the vanilla extract and all-purpose flour and mix it.
8. Add the peach mixture and walnut pieces into the mixture.
9. Add the mixture into a dish.
10. Make sure the dish is properly greased.
11. Steam your dish in a wok for fifteen to twenty minutes.
12. Dish out your peach cake.

13. Cut them into square shapes and dust the powdered sugar on top.
14. Your dish is ready to be served.

5.9 Wok Snow Fungus Soup with Pears Recipe

Preparation Time: 10 minutes
Cooking Time: 15 minutes
Serving: 2

Ingredients:

- Dried goji berries, one cup
- Dried snow fungus, one cup
- Asian pear, one
- Chinese red dates, one cup
- Water, eight cups
- Rock sugar, half cup
- Vanilla extract, one teaspoon

Instructions:
1. Take a small wok.
2. Add the water and rock sugar.
3. When the sugar dissolves in the water, add the dried goji berries, dried snow fungus, Asian pear and Chinese red dates.
4. Add the vanilla extract into the mixture.
5. Cook your mixture for approximately ten to fifteen minutes.
6. Your dish is ready to be served.

5.10 Wok Apple Cinnamon Coffee Cake Recipe

Preparation Time: 30 minutes
Cooking Time: 10 minutes
Serving: 4

Ingredients:

- Milk, two cups
- Apple slices, two
- Cinnamon, one tablespoon
- Coffee, one cup
- White sugar, half cup
- Salt, one teaspoon
- Eggs, two
- Lemon extract, one teaspoon
- Almond extract, one teaspoon
- All-purpose flour, two cups
- Butter, one cup

Instructions:
1. Take a medium bowl and add the sliced apples in it.
2. Add the coffee and cinnamon into it.
3. Add one cup flour and mix well.
4. Then refrigerate it.
5. Take a large bowl and add butter into it.
6. Add the sugar, salt and milk.
7. Mix them well.
8. Mix the warm milk mixture with the flour.
9. Add the eggs, lemon extract and almond extract together.

10. Stir it for few minutes.
11. Steam your cake in a wok for ten minutes.
12. Your dish is ready to be served.

5.11 Wok Mango Sago Recipe

Preparation Time: 10 minutes
Cooking Time: 10 minutes
Serving: 4

Ingredients:

- Milk, two cups
- Mangoes, two
- White sugar, half cup
- Salt, one teaspoon
- Eggs, two
- Lemon extract, one teaspoon
- Almond extract, one teaspoon
- All-purpose flour, two cups
- Butter, one cup

Instructions:
1. Take a medium bowl and add the mango slices in it.
2. Add the one cup flour and mix well.
3. Take a large bowl and add milk into it.
4. Add the sugar and salt as required.
5. Mix them well.
6. Mix the warm milk mixture with the flour and the yeast.

7. Add the eggs, lemon extract and almond extract together.
8. Stir it for few minutes.
9. Add the sugar to taste if required.
10. Your dish is ready to be served.

5.12 Wok Golden Syrup Recipe

Preparation Time: 30 minutes
Cooking Time: 10 minutes
Serving: 2

Ingredients:

- Boiling water, two cups
- Brown Sugar, half cup
- Baking powder, half cup
- Milk, half cup
- Salt, a pinch
- Almond extract, one tablespoon

Instructions:
1. Take a medium bowl and add the boiling water in it.
2. Add one cup flour and the rum extract.
3. Mix them well.
4. Take a large bowl and add the heavy cream into it.
5. Add the sugar, the salt and the milk.
6. Mix them well.
7. Add the eggs and the almond extract together.
8. Cook your mixture for few minutes in a wok.
9. Cook for ten minutes.

10. Your dish is ready to be served.

5.13 Wok Egg Tarts Recipe

Preparation Time: 15 minutes
Cooking Time: 25 minutes
Serving: 3

Ingredients:

- Milk, two cups
- White sugar, half cup
- Salt, one teaspoon
- Eggs, two
- Lemon extract, one teaspoon
- Almond extract, one teaspoon
- All-purpose flour, two cups
- Butter, one cup
- Dry yeast, one cup

Instructions:
1. Take a medium bowl and add the butter in it.
2. Add the one cup flour and mix well.
3. Then refrigerate it.
4. Take a large bowl and add yeast into it.
5. Add the sugar, salt and milk.
6. Mix them well.
7. Mix the warm milk mixture with the flour and the yeast.
8. Add the eggs, the lemon extract and the almond extract together.
9. Stir it for few minutes.

10. Then knead it in the flour until the dough is formed.
11. Place butter on dough and fold it in plastic wrap.
12. Refrigerate for thirty minutes.
13. Make tarts of the dough roll.
14. Steam them in a wok for ten minutes.
15. Your dish is ready to be served.

5.14 Wok Banana Bread Recipe

Preparation Time: 30 minutes
Cooking Time: 10 minutes
Serving: 4

Ingredients:

- All-purpose flour, one cup
- Mashed bananas, one cup
- Butter, half cup
- Sugar, half cup
- Baking powder, one cup
- Rum extract, one tablespoon
- Milk, one cup
- Almond extract, one tablespoon
- Heavy cream

Instructions:
1. Take a medium bowl and add the butter and mashed bananas in it.
2. Add the one cup flour and the oats.

3. Mix them well.
4. Take a large bowl and add the heavy cream into it.
5. Add the sugar, salt and milk.
6. Mix them well.
7. Add the baking powder in the mixture.
8. Add the eggs and almond extract together.
9. Stir it for few minutes.
10.   Steam the mixture in a wok for one hour.
11.   Your dish is ready to be served.

5.15 Wok Sweet Rice Balls with Black Sesame Filling Recipe

Preparation Time: 50 minutes
Cooking Time: 10 minutes
Serving: 4

Ingredients:

- Black sesame seeds, one cup
- Butter, two cups
- Warm water, half cup
- Caster sugar, one cup
- Rice flour, half cup
- Oil, one tablespoon
- Salt, to taste
- Pepper, to taste
- Ginger, two tablespoon
- Pandan leaves, three

Instructions:
1. Take four cups of water in a wok.
2. Boil the water well.
3. Add the ginger, pandan leaves and sugar.
4. Boil the water until all ingredients are dissolved.
5. Toast black sesame seeds on a wok for ten to fifteen minutes.
6. Toast the seeds until they come in a powdered form.
7. Then you can add sugar and oil as required.
8. Take a large bowl and add flour in it.
9. Make dough with your hands.
10. Cook sweet rice in the end in a large wok.
11. Fill the rice balls with black sesame seeds.
12. Cook it for ten minutes.
13. Your dish is ready to be served.

Chapter 6: The World of Traditional Wok Recipes Eaten Only by Thai People

Following are some classic traditional Thai recipes eaten only by Thai people that are rich in healthy nutrients and you can easily make them with the detailed instructions list in each recipe:

6.1 Wok Cabbage Burji Recipe

Preparation Time: 15 minutes
Cooking Time: 30 minutes
Serving: 3

Ingredients:

- Cabbage, one pound
- Carrots, one
- Tomatoes, two
- Red bell pepper, one tablespoon
- Cooking oil, one cup
- Garlic powder, one tablespoon
- Ginger, one tablespoon
- Sesame oil, one tablespoon
- Corn starch, one teaspoon
- Red chili, to serve
- Green onions, two
- Salt, to taste
- Black Pepper, to taste

Instructions:
1. Take a large wok and add oil in it.
2. Heat it over medium high heat.
3. Add the cut up cabbage into it.
4. Add the ginger, garlic powder and pepper.
5. Cook it for one minute with the continuous stirring.
6. Add the green onions into the mixture.
7. Cook it for one minute more.
8. Continue boiling for five minutes until water reduces to minimum level.
9. Add the sauce ingredients in a separate bowl.
10. Add the corn starch in the bowl.
11. Dissolve your entire cornstarch in water and make sure no lumps are formed.
12. Put the cornstarch mixture into the wok and cook well.
13. Cook until your cabbage becomes almost dry and smooth.
14. ** ** Your dish is ready to be served with the sauces that you prefer.

6.2 Wok Breakfast Poha Recipe

Preparation Time: 30 minutes
Cooking Time: 50 minutes
Serving: 5

Ingredients:

- Brown rice, one cup
- Tomatoes, two
- Red bell pepper, one tablespoon

- Cooking oil, one cup
- Garlic powder, one tablespoon
- Ginger, one tablespoon
- Sesame oil, one tablespoon
- Peanuts, one cup
- Curry leaves, three
- Cumin seeds, half tablespoon
- Red chili, to serve
- Green onions, two
- Salt, to taste
- Black Pepper, to taste

Instructions:
1. Cook the brown rice in rice cooking wok.
2. Drain the brown rice once they are cooked.
3. Add the ginger, garlic powder and pepper.
4. Cook it for one minute with continuous stirring.
5. Add the green onions into the mixture.
6. Cook it for a few minutes.
7. Add the curry leaves and cumin seeds into your mixture.
8. Add the peanuts into the dish.
9. Cook your ingredients well.
10. Add the cooked rice into whole mixture.
11. Simmer until your poha is cooked.
12. Your dish is ready to be served.

6.3 Wok Simple Millet Congee Recipe

Preparation Time: 20 minutes
Cooking Time: 20 minutes
Serving: 2

Ingredients:
- Millet, one cup
- Cream, two tablespoon
- Butter, one cup
- Eggs, two
- Cherries, two
- All-purpose flour, two cups
- Water, as required
- Baking soda, one tablespoon
- Salt, a pinch
- Pepper, to taste

Instructions:
1. Take a wok and clean it well.
2. Add the sugar and the baking soda and the millet into it.
3. Add the salt and cream.
4. Add the all-purpose flour into it so that congee can be smooth.
5. Add the crushed walnuts into the mixture.
6. Mix all the ingredients well.
7. Add beaten eggs into the mixture.
8. Pour into the dish and spread evenly.
9. Take a small bowl and add the butter.
10. Mix them until become smooth and then add it into your dish.
11. Add the salt as required.
12. Simmer it for about five minutes.
13. Your dish is ready to be served with cherries and the walnuts.

14.   You can refrigerate your dish as well.

6.4 Wok Osmanthus Cake Recipe

Preparation Time: 10 minutes
Cooking Time: 25 minutes
Serving: 3

Ingredients:
- Osmanthus syrup, one cup
- Cream, two tablespoon
- Butter, one cup
- Eggs, two
- Blueberries, half cup
- All-purpose flour, two cups
- Water, as required
- Baking soda, one tablespoon
- Salt, a pinch
- Walnuts, one cup

Instructions:
1. Take a large bowl and clean it well.
2. Add the sugar and the baking soda and the osmanthus syrup.
3. Add the salt and cream.
4. Add the all-purpose flour into it so that cake can be crispy.
5. Add the crushed walnuts into the mixture.
6. Mix all the ingredients well.
7. Add beaten eggs into the mixture.
8. Pour into the dish and spread evenly.
9. Take a small bowl and add the sugar and the butter.
10. Mix them until become smooth.
11. Add the salt as required.

12. Steam it for about twenty-five minutes.
13. Dish out your cake and then slice it.
14. Your dish is ready to be served.
15. You can refrigerate your cake as well.

6.5 Wok Chinese Sweet Peanut Cream Dessert Recipe

Preparation Time: 50 minutes
Cooking Time: 30 minutes
Serving: 4

Ingredients:
- Sweet peanuts, one cup
- Sugar, two tablespoon
- Cream, two tablespoon
- Butter, one cup
- Eggs, two
- All-purpose flour, two cups
- Water, as required
- Baking soda, one tablespoon
- Salt, a pinch

Instructions:
1. Take a large bowl and clean it well.
2. Add the sugar and the baking soda and the sweet peanuts into it.
3. Add the salt and the cream.
4. Add all-purpose flour into it so that dessert can be smooth.
5. Add the crushed peanuts and walnuts into the mixture.
6. Mix all the ingredients well.

7. Add beaten eggs into the mixture.
8. Pour into a wok and spread evenly.
9. Take a small bowl and add the sugar and the butter.
10. Mix them until the mixture becomes smooth.
11. Add the salt as required.
12. Simmer it for about twenty-five minutes.
13. Your dish is ready to be served with crushed peanuts and walnuts.
14. You can refrigerate your dessert as well.

6.6 Wok Sichuan Chicken and Vegetables Recipe

Preparation Time: 30 minutes
Cooking Time: 10 minutes
Serving: 4

Ingredients:

- Coconut cream, one cup
- Chicken stock, two cups
- Minced garlic, one teaspoon
- Minced ginger, one teaspoon
- Sichuan peppers, two tablespoon
- Shallot, one
- Kaffir lime leaves, four
- Lime wedges
- Lemon grass, two sticks
- Fish sauce, two tablespoon
- Mix vegetables, one cup
- Coconut milk, one cup
- Cilantro, a quarter cup
- Chicken pieces, half pound

- Olive oil, one tablespoon

Instructions:
1. Take a large wok.
2. Add the shallots and olive oil.
3. Cook your shallots and then add the chicken pieces.
4. When the chicken pieces are half cooked then add the chicken stock, minced garlic and ginger.
5. Add the Sichuan peppers and coconut milk.
6. Cook your ingredients until they start boiling.
7. Add in the mixed vegetables, lemon grass and rest of the ingredients into your dish.
8. Cook your ingredients for ten minutes.
9. Add the coconut cream in the end and mix it for five minutes.
10. Garnish it with cilantro leaves.
11. Your dish is ready to be served.

6.7 Wok Siri Lankan Spicy Breakfast Omelet Recipe

Preparation Time: 15 minutes
Cooking Time: 35 minutes
Serving: 2

Ingredients:

- Green onion, one cup
- Red chili, one tablespoon
- Garlic clove, one
- Mixed garam masala, one tablespoon

- Ginger, two tablespoon
- Red sauce, two tablespoon
- Eggs, three
- Tomatoes, half cup
- Softened butter, one tablespoon
- Coconut milk, one cup
- Black pepper, one tablespoon
- Salt, to taste

Instructions:
1. Take a large wok.
2. Heat your wok and add butter into the wok.
3. When the butter melts, add the chopped red onion.
4. Cook your onion and then add the mixed garam masala into the mixture.
5. Add the garlic and ginger into the wok.
6. When the color of your garlic and ginger changes, add the tomatoes into the mixture.
7. Add the red sauce, salt and black pepper into the mixture.
8. When your ingredients are cooked enough reduce the heat.
9. In a small bowl, add the eggs and coconut milk.
10. Beat your mixture well and then add it into the wok.
11. Do not mix your ingredients.
12. When the egg mixture solidifies a little, flip it over.
13. Cook both sides of your omelet to golden brown color.
14. When the eggs are done, dish them out.
15. Garnish the eggs with cilantro.
16. Your dish is ready to be served.

6.8 Wok Chinese Chili Chicken Dry Recipe

Preparation Time: 5 minutes
Cooking Time: 30 minutes
Serving: 3

Ingredients:

- Chinese chili, half cup
- Chicken, one pound
- Cornstarch, one tablespoon
- Cooking oil, half cup
- Garlic powder, one tablespoon
- Ginger, one tablespoon
- Sesame oil, one tablespoon
- Brown sugar, one cup
- Red chili, to serve
- Green onions, two
- Salt, to taste
- Black Pepper, to taste

Instructions:
1. Take a large wok and add oil in it.
2. Heat it over medium high heat.
3. Add the cut up chicken into it.
4. Add the ginger, garlic powder and pepper.
5. Cook it for one minute with the continuous stirring.
6. Add the green onions into the mixture.
7. Cook it for few more minutes.
8. Continue boiling for five minutes until water reduces to minimum level.

9. Add the sauce and the Chinese red chili in the wok.
10. Add the corn starch and brown sugar in the bowl.
11. Dissolve all the ingredients well.
12. Put all the ingredients together into the wok and cook well.
13. Cook until your chicken becomes almost dry.
14. Garnish your dish with cilantro and chili.
15. Your dish is ready to be served with the sauces that you prefer.

6.9 Wok Mongolian Chicken Recipe

Preparation Time: 5 minutes
Cooking Time: 15 minutes
Serving: 4

Ingredients:

- Chicken, one pound
- Cornstarch, one tablespoon
- Cooking oil, half cup
- Garlic powder, one tablespoon
- Ginger, one tablespoon
- Hoisin sauce, one tablespoon
- Sesame oil, one tablespoon
- Brown sugar, one cup
- Tamari sauce, half cup
- Red chili, to serve
- Green onions, two
- Salt, to taste
- Black Pepper, to taste

Instructions:
1. Take a large wok and add oil in it.
2. Heat it over medium high heat.
3. Add the cut up chicken into it.
4. Add the ginger, garlic powder and pepper.
5. Cook it for one minute with the continuous stirring.
6. Add the green onions into the mixture.
7. Cook it for a few minutes.
8. Continue boiling for five minutes until water reduces to minimum level.
9. Add the sauce ingredients in a separate bowl.
10. Add the corn starch and brown sugar in the bowl.
11. Dissolve all the ingredients well.
12. Put all the ingredients together into the wok and cook well.
13. Your dish is ready to be served with the sauces that you prefer.

6.10 Wok Chinese Omelet Recipe

Preparation Time: 15 minutes
Cooking Time: 5 minutes
Serving: 2

Ingredients:

- Green onion, one cup
- Red chili, one tablespoon
- Garlic clove, one
- Snow Peas, trimmed, one cup
- Ginger, two tablespoon

- Oyster sauce, two tablespoon
- Eggs, three
- Olive oil, two tablespoon
- Coconut milk, one cup
- Bean sprouts, one cup

Instructions:
1. Take a wok and heat it.
2. Add the snow peas into it.
3. Cover it with the boiling water for three minutes.
4. Then drain and rinse it with the cold water.
5. Take another bowl and add snow peas into it.
6. Add the bean sprouts and red chili into it and mix well.
7. Take another bowl and add a tablespoon of hot water in it.
8. Add the ginger, garlic and oyster sauce into it.
9. Combine all the ingredients well.
10. You can add pepper if you like.
11. Wash the wok and heat it.
12. Pour the egg mixture on the wok.
13. Then spread the snow pea mixture over omelet.
14. Fold the omelet and cook it on both sides.
15. When your eggs are done dish them out.
16. Your dish is ready to be served.

Conclusion

The Wok is an amazing utensil that has been used for many years in different cuisines. Indian, Chinese, Japanese, Korean and Thai cooking is deeply influenced by wok cooking. In this book, we discussed the evolution of wok cooking over the years as well as the different ingredients used while cooking food in a wok.

In this book, we have discussed different aspects of wok coking and not only the recipes. We have discussed in detail the history and origin of wok dishes. The various spices used in wok cooking have enormous amount of amazing properties that has such positive and healthy impact on our overall health. This cookbook includes 70 recipes that contain breakfast, lunch, dinner, dessert, recipes that are only eaten by Asian people. You can easily make these recipes at home without supervision of any kind. So start cooking today and enjoy cooking your food using a wok.

VEGETARIAN WOK COOKBOOK

70 Easy Recipes For Traditional Asian Food

Maki Blanc

© Copyright 2021 by (Maki Blanc) - All rights reserved.

This document is geared towards providing exact and reliable information in regards to the topic and issue covered. The publication is sold with the idea that the publisher is not required to render accounting, officially permitted, or otherwise, qualified services. If advice is necessary, legal or professional, a practiced individual in the profession should be ordered.

- From a Declaration of Principles which was accepted and approved equally by a Committee of the American Bar Association and a Committee of Publishers and Associations.

It is not legal in any way to reproduce, duplicate, or transmit any part of this document in either electronic means or in printed format. Recording of this publication is strictly prohibited and any storage of this document is not allowed unless with written permission from the publisher. All rights reserved.

The information provided herein is stated to be truthful and consistent, in that any liability, in terms of inattention or otherwise, by any usage or abuse of any policies, processes, or directions contained within is the solitary and utter responsibility of the recipient reader. Under no circumstances will any legal responsibility or blame be held against the publisher for any reparation, damages, or monetary loss due to the information herein, either directly or indirectly.

Respective authors own all copyrights not held by the publisher.

The information herein is offered for informational purposes solely, and is universal as so. The presentation of the information is without contract or any type of guarantee assurance.

The trademarks that are used are without any consent, and the publication of the trademark is without permission or backing by the trademark owner. All trademarks and brands within this book are for clarifying purposes only and are the owned by the owners themselves, not affiliated with this document.

Introduction

Wok cooking is a Chinese cooking method in which materials are mixed or flipped in a wok while still frying in a tiny portion of very hot oil. The method began in Asia and recent decades has expanded into other Asian countries and the West.

In a hot skillet or wok, wok cooking is a simple way to cook small food bites. The food is continuously stirred when cooking in a wok, as the name implies. The food is pickled when it comes into contact with the wok, which tends to lock in the flavor. Wok cooking is ideal for a wide range of foods, including meat, fish, and veggies. In contrast to deep-frying, the method uses a lot less oil. This process can be used to prepare a variety of fruits, meats, fish, and poultry.

Wok preparation is not only fast and simple, but it is also nutritious. It produces tender-crisp veggies with more nutrients than steamed veggies. The fat content is poor since wok preparation only uses a limited amount of oil.

In a skillet, which is a bowl-shaped pot, an authentic wok recipe is prepared. For mixing, you'll need a heat-resistant spoon or a big spoon. Choose a high-smoke-point oil for a wok dish since it will be cooked at elevated temperatures. This means the oil would not create any smoke or have an unpleasant odor.

Because wok-cooked foods are not heated as much as deep-fried items, they hold the majority of the nutritional values. As a consequence, this cooking process is much healthier. If you intend on doing a lot of wok preparation, make sure your workspace is well ventilated because this cooking method can produce a lot of smoke. As a result, wok dishes made with vegan products are healthier to consume.

"Vegetarian Wok Cookbook" is a complete recipe book based on all-vegetarian wok dishes from India, Japan, China, and Thailand. It has four chapters with detailed knowledge of vegetarian wok cuisine. Try these dishes at your home and make your meals more like Indians.

Chapter 1: Vegetarian Wok Indian Recipes

1.1 Indian Five-Spice Vegetable Stir-Fry

Cooking Time: 30 minutes
Serving Size: 2
   Ingredients:
   - 1 teaspoon panch phoran
   - Salt and freshly ground black pepper
   - 3 tablespoon sriracha chili sauce
   - 15g fresh coriander
   - 150g asparagus
   - 4 garlic cloves
   - 100g mange tout
   - 1 courgette
   - 1 carrot
   - 1 red pepper
   - 2 spring onions
   - 1 large red chili
   - 6 tablespoon olive oil

Method:
   1. In a skillet or a large nonstick deep fryer, heat two tablespoons of the oil over medium temperature.
   2. Stir-fry for three minutes with all the veggies except the cloves.
   3. Salt and pepper to taste.
   4. Toss the veggies with the sriracha and coriander leaves and toss well.
   5. Heat the remaining four tablespoons of olive oil in the meantime.
   6. Fry the garlic until it turns lightly browned.
   7. Warm the garlic with the Indian five-spice powder.

8. Stir in the herb and five-spice combination to coat the veggies.
9. Serve the stir-fry as soon as possible.

1.2 Wok-Seared Vegetables

Cooking Time: 35 minutes
Serving Size: 4
Ingredients:
- 1 tablespoon lime juice
- ½ cup fresh mint leaves
- 4 large cloves of garlic
- 3 dried red chilies
- 2 teaspoons coriander seeds
- 1 large green bell pepper
- 1 small red onion
- 3 tablespoons canola oil
- 2 large carrots
- 1 teaspoon cumin seeds
- ½ teaspoon ground turmeric
- 1 tablespoon cornstarch
- ¾ teaspoon salt
- 1 teaspoon fennel seeds

Method:
1. Use a spice slicer or a pestle and mortar to grind cardamom, smoked paprika, and fennel seeds.
2. Add cornflour, salt, and fenugreek to a medium mixing bowl and whisk to blend.
3. Stir in the veggies until they are evenly covered in the spice mixture.
4. Heat a large cast-iron pan or wok with a flat surface over high heat.
5. Add two tablespoon extra virgin olive oil.
6. Carrots, red pepper, cabbage, cloves, and chilies should all be added.

7. Heat, occasionally stirring, for four to eight minutes, or until the veggies begin to fry.
8. Turn down the heat to moderate and drizzle in the remaining one tablespoon of oil.
9. Heat with the ingredients from the dish.
10. Cook, constantly stirring, until the vegetables, lemon zest, and mint are heated through, around thirty seconds.

1.3 Noodles and Vegetables Stir Fry

Cooking Time: 15 minutes
Serving Size: 2
Ingredients:
- 2 tablespoon soy sauce
- 1 teaspoon white wine vinegar
- 2 spring onions
- 85g beansprout
- 150g pack egg noodle
- 1 yellow pepper
- 100g mange tout
- 1 tablespoon vegetable oil
- 2 garlic cloves
- 1 large carrot
- 2.5cm ginger

Method:
1. In a slow cooker or wide, deep fryer, add the oil, whisk the onion, ginger, cabbage, peppers, mange tout, sugar pick, or green beans for 2-3 minutes over medium temperature.
2. Drain the pasta completely, then stir-fry for two minutes with the vegetables and beansprouts.
3. Combine the sesame oil and vinegar in a mixing bowl, then mix into the skillet and stir for 1-two minutes.

4. Mix thoroughly by dividing between individual plates or cups.

1.4 Indian Stir-Fried Carrots

Cooking Time: 13 minutes
Serving Size: 4
Ingredients:
- ¼ cup coconut
- 2-3 tablespoon cilantro
- ½ teaspoon salt
- ¼ cup water
- 5 medium carrots
- 2 dried red chilies
- 1 teaspoon grated ginger
- 1-2 tablespoon olive oil
- 1 teaspoon urad dal
- 4-5 curry leaves
- 1 teaspoon whole mustard seeds

Method:
1. In a deep fryer or skillet, heat the oil until it shimmers, then insert the urad dal.
2. Add bay leaves, coriander powder, and dry bell peppers after about 20 seconds, and cook until the seeds start to pop.
3. Heat for one moment with the cut carrots, spice, and salt before adding the water.
4. Decrease to a low heat environment, cover, and boil until carrots are tender around 20 minutes.
5. Remove the lid, add the grated coconut and coriander, and toss all together.
6. Serve after tasting and adding more salt if necessary.

1.5 Vegetables in Hot Garlic Sauce

Cooking Time: 20 minutes
Serving Size: 4
   Ingredients:
Other Ingredients
- 2 tablespoon cornflour
- 4 cup water
- Salt to taste
- ½ teaspoon black pepper
- 4 whole dry red chilies
- 2 tablespoon white vinegar
- 4 tablespoon sesame oil
- 1 tablespoon ginger
- 2 tablespoon celery
- 8 -10 garlic cloves
- 2 tablespoon cooking oil

Hot Garlic Sauce
- 1 teaspoon red chili flakes
- ¼ cup red chili sauce
- 1 tablespoon brown sugar
- 2 tablespoon soy sauce

Vegetables
- 1 cup baby corn
- 1 cup zucchini
- 1 cup red bell pepper
- 1 cup mushrooms
- 1 cup green capsicum
- 1 cup yellow bell pepper
- 1 large-size onion, diced

Ingredients for Garnish
- 1 tablespoon peanuts
- 1 fresh red chili
- 1 tablespoon spring onion greens

Method:
1. Mix ½ cup water with cornflour and set aside.
2. Brown sugar, red chili flakes, sesame oil, and spicy mayo should all be combined.
3. In a broiler pan or stir-fry bowl, heat the olive oil.
4. Stir-fry all of the veggies except for the onion.
5. In the same broiler pan, warm sesame oil.
6. Add parsley, whole green chilies, pepper, and fennel, thinly sliced.
7. Stir in the diced onion for about a minute or until the onion is translucent.
8. Put in the white vinegar and thoroughly combine all of the components to glaze the plate.
9. Add the hot garlic sauce mix that has been prepared.
10. Salt and chili flakes to taste.
11. Mix in the stir-fried veggies until the sauce has thickened. Switch the heat on.
12. Add green onions, crushed peanuts, and red chili to the gravy as a garnish.

1.6 Stir-Fried Exotic Oriental Vegetable Recipe

Cooking Time: 15 minutes
Serving Size: 2

Ingredients:
- 30 ml veg stock
- 3 ml sesame oil
- 20-gram carrot
- 15 ml oyster sauce
- 30-gram bok choy
- 20-gram asparagus
- 20-gram zucchini
- 30-gram broccoli

- 2-gram sugar
- 30-gram Chinese cabbage
- 20-gram snow peas
- 10 ml virgin olive oil
- 10-gram garlic
- 30-gram mushroom

Method:
1. To start the food preparation, add the oil to the skillet and insert the minced garlic.
2. Sauté for a minimum of 30 seconds.
3. In a skillet, add blanched veggies.
4. Add sesame oil, salt, soup powder, starch, and stock after that.
5. Cook for a minute while stirring.
6. Pour sesame oil over the dish to finish it off.
7. Serve immediately on a plate with green onions as a garnish.

1.7 Potato and Green Beans Stir Fry

Cooking Time: 35 minutes
Serving Size: 5

Ingredients:
- 250 green beans
- Salt to season
- 1 teaspoon of chili fleck
- 2-3 red chilies
- 3 tablespoons of oil
- ½ teaspoon of turmeric powder
- ¼ cup water
- 2 garlic cloves
- 2 medium-sized potatoes
- 1 medium-sized onion
- A sprig of curry leaves

Method:
1. Potatoes should be cut into chunks.

2. Set down the green beans after they have been washed.
3. Position the cooking pan on the stove and add in the oil; wait a few seconds for the oil to heat up.
4. Stir in the curry leaves, tomatoes, and cloves, and cook for a few minutes.
5. To the tempering components, pour the mixture and then the turmeric powder and simmer.
6. ¼ cup water should be poured in.
7. Start to sauté with chili flakes and diced peppers.
8. Add the Brussels sprouts to the boil and sprinkle with salt.
9. Test for spice, add salt if needed, and serve hot once the bean is heated through.

1.8 Balti Stir-Fried Vegetables with Cashews

Cooking Time: 30 minutes
Serving Size: 4
   Ingredients:
   - Steamed rice
   - 50g toasted cashew nuts
   - 60 ml vegetable stock
   - 75g English spinach leaves
   - 300g slender eggplants
   - 3 ripe tomatoes
   - Two tablespoons vegetable oil
   - 70g balti curry paste
   - 1 onion

Method:
1. Heat a skillet or a deep cooking pot to a high temperature.
2. Swirl in the oil to evenly cover the side.
3. Boil the onions for 3-4 minutes over medium temperature or until translucent.

4. Heat for 1 minute after adding the curry paste, then insert the eggplant and cook over medium heat.
5. Gently throw in the tofu for four minutes or until translucent.
6. Cook for three minutes, or until the tomato is tender, after adding the tomato and stock.
7. Cook, constantly stirring, until the spinach is only wilted.
8. Season with salt and pepper to taste, then serve.

1.9 Stir-Fried Indian Okra with Spices

Cooking Time: 15 minutes
Serving Size: 4
Ingredients:
- Salt to taste
- 2 tablespoon cilantro
- 1 teaspoon amchur
- ½ teaspoon garam masala
- 1 pound okra
- ½ teaspoon turmeric
- ½ teaspoon paprika
- 1 tablespoon vegetable oil
- 1 green chili pepper
- 1 tablespoon coriander powder
- 2 cloves garlic
- ½ inch ginger
- 1 medium onion
- 2 medium tomatoes
- 1 teaspoon cumin seeds

Method:
1. Position the okra in a steamer basket with ½ teaspoon of oil.
2. For an 8-minute air fried, preheat the oven to 375°F.

3. In a skillet, heat the remaining oil.
4. Transfer the cumin seeds and a bit of salt after they have darkened slightly.
5. Sauté the vegetables until they are transparent and starting to brown.
6. Combine the ginger, cloves, and green hot peppers in a mixing bowl.
7. Mix in the tomatoes, then insert the seasoning.
8. Put a cup of water to a boil with the onions and tomatoes.
9. Sprinkle with salt and transfer the okra that has been prepared to the sauce.
10. Serve immediately with a garnish of cilantro.

1.10 Vegetable Jalfrezi

Cooking Time: 15 minutes
Serving Size: 4

Ingredients:
- Few mint leaves
- 3 tablespoon oil divided
- 1 teaspoon garam masala
- 1 tablespoon white vinegar
- ¾ cup bell peppers
- 2 tablespoon red chili powder
- Salt to taste
- ½ cup carrots and string beans
- 1 teaspoon cumin seeds
- 1 teaspoon onion seeds
- ½ cup cauliflower florets
- 1 cup diced tomatoes
- Few shreds of ginger
- ½ cup paneer
- ¾ cup onions

Method:

1. Heat the vegetables, green beans, and florets for five minutes in hot water.
2. In a skillet, heat ½ teaspoon oil.
3. Sauté the paneer pieces until golden brown.
4. In the same bowl, add around ½ teaspoon oil and the vegetables and bell peppers.
5. In the same pan, make two tablespoons of oil.
6. Insert the cumin and onion seeds when the pan is heated.
7. Cook until the tomatoes are mushy and the oil extracts, then add the diced tomatoes.
8. Combine the paprika, curry powder, and salt in a cup.
9. Combine the onion-pepper mixture and the sautéed veggies in a large mixing bowl.
10. Combine the ground ginger and the vinegar in a mixing bowl. Combine all of the ingredients, including the paneer that has been sautéed.
11. Heat to a high temperature. Serve with the mint leaves.

1.11 Quinoa Fried Rice Recipe

Cooking Time: 30 minutes
Serving Size: 4

Ingredients:
- 3 large eggs
- Thinly sliced green onions
- 2 cloves garlic
- 2 tablespoon soy sauce
- 1 cup quinoa
- 1 large carrot
- 1 ½ cup frozen peas
- 1 tablespoon. sesame oil
- 1 large onion
- Kosher salt

Method:
1. Take 2 cups of water and brown rice to a boil in a small saucepan.
2. Cover and simmer for 20 minutes, or until all of the water has been absorbed.
3. Fluff with a fork after seasoning with salt.
4. Add the oil to a large frying pan.
5. Cook, occasionally stirring, until the onion, carrot, and peas are tender around 10 to 15 minutes.
6. Cook for another minute until the garlic and soy sauces are fragrant.
7. Scramble the eggs for 1 to 2 minutes.
8. Three minutes after adding the cooked quinoa, heat completely.
9. Cover with spring onions and rain of sesame oil.

1.12 Chili Paneer

Cooking Time: 30 minutes
Serving Size: 3

Ingredients:
For Paneer Pakoda
- 9 cubes paneer
- Oil for deep frying
- ½ teaspoon ginger-garlic paste
- ¼ cup water
- 1 teaspoon soy sauce
- ¼ teaspoon salt
- ¼ cup cornflour
- ½ teaspoon pepper
- ½ teaspoon red chili powder
- ¼ cup all-purpose flour

For Gravy
- 1 tablespoon cornflour
- 1 cup water
- ¼ teaspoon pepper
- ¼ teaspoon salt
- 4 teaspoon oil
- 2 tablespoon soy sauce
- 1 tablespoon chili sauce
- ½ capsicum
- 2 tablespoon vinegar
- 2 cloves garlic
- 2 tablespoon onion
- 2 green chili
- 4 tablespoon spring onion

Method:
1. To begin, make a corn flour batter with seasoning.

2. Paneer pieces are then dipped in egg and deep-fried in hot oil.
3. Fry the paneer until golden brown and crispy.
4. Heat 4 teaspoon oil and sauté cloves to make the gravy.
5. Spring tomato, onion, and green chili are also good additions.
6. In addition, insert ½ capsicum and gently sauté.
7. Add vinegar, sesame oil, chili sauce, pepper, and salt to taste.
8. Cook over high heat until the mixture thickens.
9. Pour in the cornflour water and keep stirring.
10. Add the paneer that has been fried.
11. Finally, prepare the fried rice with the chili paneer gravy.

1.13 Frozen Mixed Vegetable Fry

Cooking Time: 10 minutes
Serving Size: 6
Ingredients:
- 1 package frozen vegetables
- 2 tablespoons soy sauce
- 2 teaspoons peanut butter
- 1 tablespoon brown sugar
- 2 teaspoons garlic powder
- 2 teaspoons olive oil

Method:
1. In a shallow saucepan, mix soy sauce, garlic powder, red pepper, and cottage cheese.
2. In a medium saucepan, heat the oil over moderate heat and cook and stir the fresh veggies until they are just tender around 6 to 10 minutes.
3. Remove the pan from the heat and stir in the soy sauce combination.

1.14 Curry Fried Rice

Cooking Time: 30 minutes
Serving Size: 4
  Ingredients:
- ¼ cup scallions
- Freshly parsley
- ½ cup frozen corn
- Kosher salt and black pepper
- 2 tablespoon Tamari
- ½ cup frozen peas
- 2 eggs
- 1.5 tablespoon curry powder
- 1 large carrot
- 1 cup mushrooms
- 4 cups cooked rice
- 1 yellow onion
- 1 rib of celery
- 3 garlic cloves
- 2 tablespoon olive oil

Method:
1. In a medium saucepan or skillet, heat the oil over medium heat.
2. Simmer with the onions and garlic.
3. Combine the celery, broccoli, and herbs in a large mixing bowl.
4. Add the garam masala, kosher salt, and salt and pepper to taste.
5. Wipe the veggies to the bottom of the plate; if necessary, add a little more oil. In the middle of the plate, pour the egg mixture.
6. In quantities, add the rice to the pan and whisk to coat.
7. Mix in the tamari or soy sauce thoroughly.

8. Insert the green onion, green beans, and canned corn at the top.
9. Reduce the heat to low and gently press the rice into a bowl.
10. If required, season with salt and black pepper.
11. Serve immediately after removing the skillet from the heat and garnishing it with freshly grated parmesan.

1.15 South Indian Brinjal Stir Fry

Cooking Time: 35 minutes
Serving Size: 4

Ingredients:
- 2 teaspoons salt
- 1–2 teaspoons red chili powder
- 1 teaspoon urad dal
- 1 teaspoon asafetida powder
- 5 tablespoon vegetable oil
- 1 teaspoon mustard seeds
- 1 onion
- 8–10 ripe brinjal

Method:
1. Rinse the brinjal thoroughly. Remove the ends.
2. Cut the eggplant in half lengthwise.
3. Place the diced pieces in the water-filled bowl.
4. In a saute pan or skillet, heat the oil.
5. Toss in the mustard seeds.
6. Roast for 20 seconds with the urad dal and asafetida.
7. In the same pan, insert the brinjal pieces.
8. Heat the stove to a low heat setting and cover the pan with water.
9. Mix in the salt and onions thoroughly.
10. Shut the cover and continue cooking.

11. Every 2-3 minutes, give it a swirl.
12. Mix in the red chili powder thoroughly.
13. Stir fry for 3-4 minutes more. Turn off the stove.

1.16 Indian-Spiced Pickled Vegetables

Cooking Time: 30 minutes
Serving Size: 4
  Ingredients:
- ½ cup distilled white vinegar
- 3 tablespoons brown sugar
- 1/3 cup vegetable oil
- 5 dried hot red chili
- ½ seedless cucumber
- ½ teaspoon cumin seeds
- ½ teaspoon fennel seeds
- 1 teaspoon coriander seeds
- 1 teaspoon ground turmeric
- ½ large head cauliflower
- 3 tablespoons peeled ginger
- 1 tablespoon mustard seeds
- 3 tablespoons garlic
- ½ lb. carrots

Method:
1. Preheat the oven to 250°F and place the rack in the center.
2. In a big pot of hot simmering water, cook the cabbage and carrots along.
3. Bake, mixing periodically, cabbage, carrots, and celery in a single layer in a shallow baking tray.
4. In a mixing bowl, pulse cloves and spice with one teaspoon of salts until golden brown, then move to a cup.
5. Heat skillet over medium temperature until a drop of water evaporates in a matter of seconds.

6. Pour the oil down the side of the skillet.
7. Cook, mixing, for ten seconds after adding the chili and spice mixture.
8. Heat, constantly stirring, until the garlic paste turns golden, around 15 seconds.
9. Bring the vegetables, mustard, and brown sugar to a boil.
10. Enable to solidify at room temperature in a small bowl.

1.17 Cashew Chickpea Curry

Cooking Time: 30 minutes
Serving Size: 4
  Ingredients:
  For the Spice Mix
- ½ teaspoon turmeric
- 1 green cardamom pod
- ¼ teaspoon nutmeg
- 1 blade mace
- 1½ teaspoons cumin seeds
- ½ teaspoon peppercorns
- ½ teaspoon cinnamon
- 1 whole star anise
- 2 cloves
- 1½ teaspoons coriander seeds

For the Curry
- ¼ cup fresh juice limes
- ½ cup fresh cilantro
- 1 bunch spinach leaves
- Kosher salt
- 3 tablespoons vegetable oil
- 1 can coconut milk
- 2 cans chickpeas
- 1 small onion
- ¼ teaspoon cayenne pepper
- ½ cup cashew nuts
- 1 tablespoon ginger
- 1 small red or green chili
- 4 cloves garlic

Method:
1. In a seasoning grinder, mix cumin, cilantro, star anise, garlic, peppercorns, cloves, nutmeg, mace, fenugreek, and cinnamon.
2. In a medium skillet, melt the oil, butter, or peanut oil over moderate flame.
3. Combine the onion, garlic, spice, and chili in a large mixing bowl.
4. Add the cayenne pepper, cashews, and half of the spice mixture to the pan.
5. Cook, stirring continuously until the mixture becomes fragrant.
6. Remove the pan from the heat and add the coconut milk.
7. Blend for around thirty seconds or until smooth.
8. Put the mixture back in the pot.
9. Cook, mixing continuously for ten minutes over low heat with chickpeas, broccoli, and the remaining spice mix.
10. To taste, season with salt and lemon juice.
11. Serve with lime slices and curry powder pilaf in a serving dish, topped with extra coriander.

1.18 Stir-Fried Chili Greens

Cooking Time: 40 minutes
Serving Size: 3

Ingredients:
- 100g frozen peas
- ½ lemon, juiced
- 1 tablespoon ginger
- 1 red chili
- 1 green chili
- 450g sliced greens
- 1 teaspoon cumin seeds

- 1 teaspoon mustard seeds
- 1 tablespoon vegetable oil

Method:
1. In a resealable roasting pan set over a moderate flame, add the oil.
2. Heat for 1 minute after adding the cumin and mustard seeds, then insert the chili and spice and cook for 30 seconds.
3. Combine the vegetables, peas, three tablespoons of water, and a bit of salt in a large mixing bowl.
4. Cook for five minutes with the lid on. To eat, sprinkle with lemon juice.

Chapter 2: Vegetarian Wok Japanese Recipes

2.1 Yasai Itame

Cooking Time: 15 minutes
Serving Size: 4
Ingredients:
- 1 tablespoon neutral oil
- 3.5 oz. bean sprouts
- 1 clove garlic
- 1 knob ginger
- 6.5 oz. pork
- ¼ cabbage
- ½ carrot
- ¼ onion
- 10 snow peas

For Pork Marinade
- 1 teaspoon sake
- 1 teaspoon soy sauce

For Seasonings
- Freshly ground black pepper
- 2 teaspoon sesame oil
- 1 teaspoon soy sauce
- ½ teaspoon kosher salt
- 1 teaspoon oyster sauce

Method:
1. Slice the vegetables into tiny chunks and sauté them in a shallow saucepan with one teaspoon sesame oil and one teaspoon sake.
2. Start by removing the strings from the green beans and thinly slice the red pepper.
3. Add the ginger and garlic once the wok is warmed.

4. When the meat is fragrant, insert it and prepare until it's around 80% cooked.
5. Stir in the onion and cook until it is almost tender. After that, add the carrots.
6. Combine the broccoli and snow peas in a large mixing bowl.
7. Then throw in the bean sprouts one more period.
8. Combine the oyster sauce and sesame oil in a bowl.
9. Add Salt, fresh roasted black pepper, and two teaspoons of sesame oil to taste.

2.2 Japanese Stir-Fried Noodles with Veggies

Cooking Time: 30 minutes
Serving Size: 3
Ingredients:
- 2 teaspoon soy sauce
- 2 teaspoon sugar
- 4 teaspoon oyster sauce
- 4 teaspoon ketchup
- ½ onion
- 1 carrot
- 4-6 tablespoon yakisoba sauce
- 4 tablespoon Worcestershire sauce
- 3 shiitake mushrooms
- Freshly ground black pepper
- 3 servings of yakisoba noodles
- 2 green onions
- ¾ lb. sliced pork belly
- 2 tablespoon neutral-flavored oil
- 4 cabbage leaves

Method:
1. Gather all of the necessary ingredients.
2. To make the Yakisoba paste, whisk together all of the components.
3. Break the onion into slices, the carrot into diced pieces, and the shiitake mushrooms into chunks.

4. Heat the oil in a pan or skillet over moderate flame.
5. Cook the vegetables until it is wilted in the center.
6. Cook for 1-2 minutes after adding the onion and carrots.
7. Cook till the cabbage is almost soft.
8. Heat for 1 minute after adding the spring onions and butternut squash.
9. Season with smoked paprika, fresh roasted.
10. Add the Yakisoba Sauce and change the quantity depending on the rest of the ingredients. Serve right away.

2.3 Lightly Fried Japanese Vegetables

Cooking Time: 50 minutes
Serving Size: 4
   Ingredients:
- Sea salt
- Toasted sesame seeds
- 2 teaspoons mirin
- Sesame oil
- ¼ white cabbage
- 1 tablespoon rice wine vinegar
- 1 tablespoon tamari
- 2 carrots
- 1 small red bell pepper
- 1 small white onion
- 4 spring onions
- 1 zucchini

Method:
1. Over medium temperature, heat a big skillet.
2. Add the soy sauce and the veggies once the soy sauce has reached a Smokey flavor.
3. Mix the rice sherry vinegar, tamari, and mirin in a small mixing bowl.
4. To add moisture to the veggies, spray the combination over them when stir-frying.

5. Heat for two minutes, testing to see if the veggies are still crisp.
6. Dress with sea salt if desired, then arrange on serving trays with toasted pine nuts on top.

2.4 Vegan Stir-Fried Udon Noodles

Cooking Time: 15 minutes
Serving Size: 4
  Ingredients:
- ¼ cup water
- 10.6 ounces Udon noodles
- 1 teaspoon ground ginger
- 4 tablespoon tamari
- 1 tablespoon olive oil
- 1 cup green pepper
- 1 cup carrot
- 1 cup red pepper
- 1 cup onion

Method:
1. In a skillet, heat the oil, add vegetables, fresh ginger, 2 tablespoons soya sauce or sesame oil, and liquid.
2. Cook for five minutes on high heat or until the vegetables are cooked.
3. Cook Udon pasta as directed on the box.
4. Two tablespoons of veggie broth or soy sauce, plus the pasta.
5. Cook for another two minutes, stirring occasionally.

2.5 Vegetable Yakisoba

Cooking Time: 40 minutes
Serving Size: 10

Ingredients:
- 16 oz. yakisoba noodles
- 3 tablespoon oil
- ¼ small cabbage
- 1 large onion
- ½ lb. broccoli
- 2 large carrots
- 1 large sweet bell pepper

Yakisoba Sauce
- 2 tablespoon ketchup
- 4 tablespoon Worcestershire sauce
- 2 tablespoon soy sauce
- 2 tablespoon oyster sauce
- 2 tablespoon sugar

Method:
1. Mix all yakisoba liquid ingredients in a large bowl and set aside.
2. Heat a small amount of oil in a skillet over high heat.
3. Return all of the veggies to the same pan. Separate the noodles as directed on the box. Toss in the noodles in the skillet.
4. Toss all together after pouring the sauce over the components.
5. Reduce the heat to medium-low and cook for five minutes.
6. Take it off the heat and enjoy it!

2.6 Hibachi Vegetables

Cooking Time: 20 minutes
Serving Size: 4
  Ingredients:
- ½ teaspoon sesame seeds
- Salt and pepper to taste
- 1 tablespoon soy sauce
- 2 tablespoons teriyaki sauce
- 2 cups broccoli florets
- 8 oz. mushrooms
- 2 tablespoons butter
- 1 zucchini
- 1 cup carrots
- ½ tablespoon garlic
- ½ sweet onion
- 1 tablespoon oil

Method:
1. Melt butter in a skillet over medium-high heat, then add the oil and sauté tomatoes and ginger for two minutes, until it's tender.
2. Zucchini, cabbage, lettuce, and mushrooms are all good additions.
3. Dress with salt and pepper to taste after adding the sesame oil and teriyaki sauce.
4. Cook for ten minutes, or until the vegetables are tender.
5. Serve immediately with toasted pine nuts scattered on top.

2.7 Wagamama Wok-Fried Greens

Cooking Time: 20 minutes

Serving Size: 2
Ingredients:
For the Sauce
- 1 tablespoon sesame oil
- Ground black pepper
- 1 teaspoon sugar
- 2 tablespoons soy sauce

For the Greens
- 150g tender stem broccoli
- 200g pak choi
- 2 garlic cloves
- 2 tablespoons oil

Method:
1. In a small mixing bowl, combine all of the sauce components.
2. In a slow cooker or cooking pan, add the oil.
3. Fry the garlic for about thirty seconds on medium heat until aromatic and golden brown – be careful not to damage it!
4. Combine the broccoli, bok choy, and liquid in a large mixing bowl.
5. Heat, frequently stirring, for around five minutes, or until veggies are cooked to your taste.
6. Taste, and if possible, add more soy sauce.

2.8 Vegan Mapo Nasu

Cooking Time: 30 minutes
Serving Size: 6
Ingredients:
- ½ cup slivered scallions
- Cilantro sprigs
- 1 teaspoon Sichuan pepper
- 1 tablespoon corn starch
- 8 ounces shiitake mushrooms
- 2 teaspoons soy sauce
- 1 teaspoon sesame oil

- 2 teaspoons garlic
- 1 tablespoon ginger
- 1 tablespoon black beans
- 1 tablespoon broad bean paste
- 2 cups water
- 3 tablespoons vegetable oil
- 3 small red peppers
- Salt
- 15-ounce soft tofu

Method:
1. Mushroom stems should be removed.
2. Simmer the stems in 2 cups water for fifteen minutes to make a light mushrooms soup.
3. Tofu should be sliced into 1-inch pieces.
4. In a pan or a large skillet, heat the oil over medium-high heat.
5. Heat, occasionally stirring, until the red peppers, bean sprouts, and bean paste are spicy, around 1 minute.
6. Stir in the ginger and garlic, and add the mushroom, sesame oil, soy sauce, and Sichuan pepper.
7. Toss in the tofu cubes with care.
8. Sprinkle in the cornstarch combination, stirring the pan gently to mix it.
9. Add green onion and coriander sprigs to finish.

2.9 15 Minute Spicy Udon Stir Fry

Cooking Time: 15 minutes
Serving Size: 2
   Ingredients:
   Stir Fry
- 3 cups baby spinach

- 14 oz. soft udon noodles
- 1 medium carrot
- 1 cup green onion
- ½ medium onion
- 1 tablespoon vegetable oil

Sauce
- 2 cloves garlic
- 1 teaspoon sesame oil
- 2 tablespoon brown sugar
- 1 tablespoon fresh ginger
- ¼ cup soy sauce
- 2 teaspoon rice wine vinegar
- 2 teaspoon Sambal Oelek

For Garnish
- Additional green onion
- ¼ cup parsley
- Sesame seeds

Method:
1. Put down your veggies after they've been prepared.
2. In a shallow saucepan, combine all of the ingredients to make the sauce.
3. Heat the oil in a large skillet pot or broiler over medium-high heat until it is hot.
4. Cook, occasionally stirring, for about a minute after adding the carrots.
5. Cook, regularly mixing, until vegetables are soft and carrots are ready.
6. Cook for thirty seconds or so, stirring occasionally.
7. Cook, tossing, for thirty seconds or so after adding the soaked noodles to the wok.
8. Reheat for another thirty seconds, constantly stirring to ensure that everything is well combined.
9. Switch the stir fry to a cup or plate and sprinkle sesame seeds on top.

2.10 Stir-Fried Tofu with Vegetables

Cooking Time: 50 minutes
Serving Size: 4
Ingredients:
For Tofu
- ½ teaspoon black pepper
- 2 tablespoon cornstarch
- 1 tablespoon soy sauce
- 1 tablespoon sesame oil
- 1 block extra-firm tofu

For Stir Fry
- 1 red bell pepper
- 2 green onions
- 2 small carrots
- 1 small head of broccoli
- 3 tablespoon olive oil
- 1 tablespoon ginger
- 8 oz. string beans
- 3 cloves garlic
- Kosher salt

For Sauce
- 2 tablespoon brown sugar
- 2 teaspoon cornstarch
- 2 teaspoon sesame oil
- ¼ cup water
- 2 tablespoon soy sauce

Method:
1. Tofu should be simmered for two minutes in a small saucepan of lightly salted water.
2. Toss tofu in a mixing saucepan with sesame oil, soy sauce, and chili flakes after cutting it into bite-size bits.
3. Add the oil to a large frying pan. Allow tofu to bake.
4. Take from pan and season with salt and pepper before setting aside.

5. Cook until the residual oil is hot, then add the ginger and garlic and fry until aromatic.
6. String bean, broccoli, lettuce, bell pepper, and fresh basil should all be added at this stage. Salt and pepper to taste.
7. Combine soy sauce, soy sauce, water, coconut milk, and cornflour in a small cup.
8. Return the tofu to the skillet and insert the sauce combination.
9. Mix and cook for 2 minutes, or until slightly boiled.

2.11 Japanese Mushroom Stir-Fry

Cooking Time: 10 minutes
Serving Size: 2

Ingredients:
- 2 tablespoon fermented soybeans
- 8 shiitake mushrooms
- 1 small eggplant
- 1 clove garlic
- 2 tablespoon vegetable oil
- 1 x 2cm piece of ginger

Sauce
- 1 tablespoon mirin
- 1 tablespoon miso paste
- 1 tablespoon soy sauce
- ½ teaspoon sesame oil
- 2 teaspoon sugar

Method:
1. Whisk together all of the sauce components.
2. In a warm skillet, add oil and the garlic and ginger, and fry until translucent.
3. Toss the veggies in the skillet with the oil.
4. Toss in the sliced eggplant and mushrooms for two minutes, just until the eggplant softens.
5. Toss in the liquid, bring to the boil, and toss once more.

6. Turn off the heat after adding the soybeans and tossing them through.
7. Serve hot with beans.

2.12 Veggie Stir-Fry Soba Noodle

Cooking Time: 15 minutes
Serving Size: 1
Ingredients:
- 1 tablespoon Sriracha sauce
- 1 tablespoon creamy nut butter
- 1 large egg
- 1 tablespoon coconut amino
- ¼ cup bell pepper
- ¼ cup broccoli florets
- ½ teaspoon ground ginger
- ¼ cup onion
- ½ tablespoon sesame oil
- ½ teaspoon garlic
- 2 ounces soba noodles

Method:
1. Take a medium pot half-filled with water on the stove.
2. Use the soba pasta in the broth.
3. In a medium saucepan, heat the soy sauce over medium-high heat.
4. Combine the ginger, onions, red pepper, garlic, and vegetables in a large mixing bowl.
5. Wrap the pan and bake, stirring periodically, for approximately 3 minutes, or until melted.
6. Strain the soba pasta and toss them in the pan with the veggies.
7. Push all to the sides, cut yolk and white with a fork until scrambled, and then fold into the veggies and pasta.
8. Add in the Sriracha, coconut protein, and almond butter until thoroughly mixed. Heat the pan before serving.

2.13 Speedy Japanese Miso Stir Fry & Sticky Rice

Cooking Time: 20 minutes
Serving Size: 2
   Ingredients:
   - 90g pack bok choy
   - 6 spring onions
   - 1 tablespoon sunflower oil
   - 250g broccoli
   - 1 tablespoon sesame seed
   - 1 teaspoon sesame oil
   - 140g sushi rice
   - 1 tablespoon caster sugar

For the Sauce
   - 2 teaspoon ginger
   - 1 red chili
   - 1 tablespoon rice wine vinegar
   - 1 tablespoon soft brown sugar
   - 1 tablespoon mirin
   - 2 tablespoon brown miso paste

Method:
1. Combine all of the sauce components in a mixing bowl with 1 tablespoon water.
2. With the icing salt and sugar, bring a big pot of water to a boil.
3. Cook for fifteen minutes after adding the rice.
4. Cap and keep warm by sprinkling the sesame seeds and sesame oil on top.
5. In a skillet, heat the essential oils until very warm, then mix in the lettuce and stir-fry for three minutes, or until nearly tender, inserting splatters of water to produce steam as required.

6. Cook for another 1-2 minutes after adding the bok choy and spring vegetables, then whisk in the sauce.
7. Divide the rice between two bowls, top with the stir-fry, and serve right away.

2.14 Japanese Shrimp & Eggplant Fried Rice

Cooking Time: 35 minutes
Serving Size: 4
Ingredients:
- 2 cups brown rice
- ¼ cup ponzu sauce
- 2 cups eggplant
- 1 cup shelled edamame
- 2 teaspoons garlic
- 1 pound raw shrimp
- 3 scallions
- 2 teaspoons ginger
- 2 large eggs
- 1 teaspoon peanut oil

Method:
1. In a big flat-bottomed wok, warm 1 teaspoon oil.
2. Heat without mixing the eggs.
3. 1 tablespoon oil, green onions, garlic, and cloves in a skillet; cook, swirling, once scallions are soft.
4. Cook for two minutes, stirring constantly.
5. Cook the eggplant and edamame together.
6. Fill a big plate halfway with the contents of the skillet.
7. In the same wok, add the rest one tablespoon oil; add the rice and swirl until it is sweet.
8. Transfer the seafood, vegetables, and shells to the skillet, along with the ponzu sauce, and stir properly.

2.15 Vegan Ramen

Cooking Time: 20 minutes

Serving Size: 3
Ingredients:
- ½ a red pepper
- ½ a zucchini
- 2 carrots
- ½ head of broccoli
- 2 cloves of garlic
- 2 green onions
- 2 tablespoon flavored oil
- 1 tablespoon ginger
- 2 packages of ramen noodles

For the Stir Fry Sauce
- 1 tablespoon sriracha
- 1 ½ teaspoons cornstarch
- 3 tablespoons soy sauce
- 1 ½ tablespoons molasses
- 2 tablespoons vegetable stock

Method:
1. For the pasta, bring a pot of water to a boil.
2. In the meantime, chop all of your vegetables and mix the stir fry sauce ingredients.
3. Insert the noodles once the water has reached a boil.
4. In a wok or wide pan, add the oil over moderate flame.
5. Combine the ginger, cloves, and the white and light green portions of the spring onions in a mixing bowl.
6. Fry for 10-15 seconds, moving continuously.
7. Combine the broccoli and vegetables in a large mixing bowl.
8. Stir fry until the vegetables start to soften.
9. Continue to stir fry the bell pepper and zucchini.
10. Pour the sauce over the pasta in the bowl.
11. Serve with the green tips of the spring onions.

2.16 Vegetable Lo Mein

Cooking Time: 25 minutes
Serving Size: 4
Ingredients:
- ½ cup snow peas
- 3 cups baby spinach
- 1 red bell pepper
- 1 carrot
- 8 ounces egg noodles
- 2 cloves garlic
- 2 cups cremini mushrooms
- 1 tablespoon olive oil

For the Sauce
- ½ teaspoon ground ginger
- ½ teaspoon Sriracha
- 2 teaspoons sugar
- 1 teaspoon sesame oil
- 2 tablespoons soy sauce

Method:
1. Set down a bowl full containing sesame oil, sugar, soy sauce, spice, and Sriracha.
2. Heat pasta as per package directions in a large pot of water; rinse well.
3. In a medium saucepan or skillet, heat the olive oil over medium heat.
4. Garlic, onions, red pepper, and carrot are added to the pan.
5. Mix in the green beans and spinach for around 2-3 minutes, or until the kale has ripened.
6. Toss in the egg noodles with the soy sauce combination and toss gently to blend.
7. Serve right away.

2.17 Szechuan Eggplant

Cooking Time: 45 minutes
Serving Size: 4
   Ingredients:
- 2 teaspoons ginger
- 10 dried red chilies
- 4 tablespoons peanut oil
- 4 cloves garlic
- 2 teaspoons salt
- 2 tablespoons cornstarch
- 1½ lbs. Japanese Eggplant

Szechuan Sauce
- 3 tablespoons sugar
- ½ teaspoon five-spice
- 1 tablespoon rice vinegar
- 1 tablespoon cooking wine
- 1 teaspoon Szechuan peppercorns
- 1 tablespoon garlic chili paste
- 1 tablespoon sesame oil
- ¼ cup soy sauce

Method:
1. Cut the eggplant into ½ inch slices.
2. Place in a large mixing bowl with two teaspoons salts and fill with water.
3. Meanwhile, finely cut the ginger and garlic.
4. In a dry pan, toast the Szechuan peppers.
5. In a small cup, whisk together these and the leftover marinade.
6. Combine the eggplant and corn starch in a mixing bowl.
7. In an extra-large pan, heat 1 to 2 teaspoons oil over moderate flame.
8. Half of the eggplant should be spread out.
9. Add one tablespoon of further oil to the skillet and cook the ginger and garlic for two minutes over low heat, stirring constantly.

10. Serve in a casserole plate with shallots on top.

Chapter 3: Vegetarian Wok Chinese Recipes

3.1 Saucy Vegetable Stir Fry

Cooking Time: 15 minutes
Serving Size: 4
Ingredients:
- 1 cup mushrooms
- 1 capsicum
- 1 carrot
- 3 medium bok choy
- 1 tablespoon vegetable oil
- 1 tablespoon ginger
- ½ onion
- 2 garlic cloves

Sauce
- Dash of white pepper
- ¾ cup water
- 1 tablespoon Chinese cooking wine
- ½ teaspoon sesame oil
- 1½ tablespoon soy sauce
- 2 teaspoon Oyster Sauce
- 1 tablespoon cornflour

Method:
1. In a mixing bowl, whisk together the cornflour and soy sauce till the cornflour is dissolved completely, then add the remaining sauce components.
2. In a skillet or a large heavy-bottomed skillet, heat the oil over medium temperature.
3. Stir in the ginger and garlic for ten seconds.
4. Stir in the onion for thirty seconds.
5. Stir in the carrots, bell pepper, and bok choy stems for two minutes.

6. Mix in the mushrooms for two or three minutes, or until the veggies are almost finished.
7. Toss in the Sauce for two minutes, or until it thickens and becomes shiny.
8. Remove the pan from the heat and serve over rice.

3.2 Vegetable Stir-Fry Noodles

Cooking Time: 10 minutes
Serving Size: 2

Ingredients:
- 2 tablespoon soy sauce
- 1 teaspoon white wine vinegar
- 2 spring onions
- 85g beansprout
- 150g pack egg noodle
- 1 yellow pepper
- 100g mange tout
- 1 tablespoon vegetable oil
- 2 garlic cloves
- 1 large carrot
- 2.5cm ginger

Method:
1. Cook the noodles as directed on the package.
2. In a griddle or large deep fryer, add the oil, whisk the onion, ginger, cabbage, peppers, mange tout, sweet snap, or green beans for 2-3 minutes over medium temperature.
3. Drain the pasta thoroughly, then stir-fry for two minutes with the vegetables and beansprouts, if using.
4. Combine the sesame oil and mustard in a bowl and stir into the dish.
5. Serve immediately after dividing between plates.

3.3 Ginger Veggie Stir Fry

Cooking Time: 40 minutes

Serving Size: 6
Ingredients:
- ¼ cup onion
- ½ tablespoon salt
- 2 tablespoons soy sauce
- 2 ½ tablespoons water
- ¾ cup carrots
- ½ cup green beans
- 1 tablespoon cornstarch
- 1 small head of broccoli
- ½ cup snow peas
- 1 ½ cloves garlic
- ¼ cup vegetable oil
- 2 teaspoons ginger root

Method:
1. Mix cornflour, cloves, one teaspoon ginger, and two tablespoons of veggie butter in a pan mixing bowl until cornstarch is absorbed.
2. Toss in the tomatoes, snow peas, vegetables, and sweet potatoes, lightly coating them.
3. In a medium saucepan or Dutch oven, heat the remaining two tablespoons of oil over medium-high heat.
4. Cook for an additional minute in oil with the vegetables.
5. Combine the soy sauce and liquid in a mixing bowl.
6. Combine the onion, salt, and the leftover one teaspoon ginger in a mixing bowl.
7. Cook until the veggies are soft but still crispy, about 10 minutes.

3.4 Stir-Fried Lettuce with Garlic Chiles

Cooking Time: 15 minutes
Serving Size: 3
Ingredients:
- 2 teaspoons oyster sauce

- 1 teaspoon salt
- 4 cloves garlic
- 1 head romaine lettuce
- 2 spring onions
- 1 ½ tablespoon vegetable oil

Method:
1. In a slow cooker or big skillet, add the oil over medium heat and add the spring onions and half of the seasoning.
2. Continue cooking for 1 minute, or until moist.
3. Continue cooking in the romaine lettuce and miso paste until the basil turns greenish.
4. Reduce the heat to moderate.
5. Stir in the leftover garlic and salt to the lettuce combination.

3.5 Wok Black Bean Glaze and Tossed Veggies in Honey Recipe

Cooking Time: 25 minutes
Serving Size: 4

Ingredients:
- 1 tablespoon honey
- 1 teaspoon black pepper
- 1 ½ teaspoon bean and garlic paste
- ½ lime
- 4-5 sweet gourds
- 4-5 water chestnuts
- 1 teaspoon soya sauce
- 1 medium Chinese cabbage
- To taste salt
- 4-5 shitake mushrooms
- 1 teaspoon ginger
- 1 bok choy

Method:
1. In a skillet, put a tablespoon of oil, transfer all the diced vegetables to it.

2. Season with salt and pepper.
3. Water cucumbers and shitake mushrooms should be added at this stage.
4. Vegetable oil, sweet potato and garlic paste, ½ lime juice, sugar, and crushed black pepper are added.
5. In a skillet, mix thoroughly for around 4-5 minutes. Serve immediately.

3.6 Shrimp and Chinese Vegetable Stir-Fry

Cooking Time: 10 minutes
Serving Size: 3
Ingredients:
- 3 button mushrooms
- 6 snow peas
- ¼ yellow bell pepper
- 4 asparagus
- 20 shrimp
- A small pinch of salt
- ½ tablespoon sesame oil
- Three tablespoons vegetable cooking oil
- 1 tablespoon fish sauce
- 2 cloves garlic

Marinating
- ¼ teaspoon sugar
- ¼ teaspoon ground white pepper
- ¼ teaspoon salt

Method:
1. Devein the shrimp and season with salt, sea salt, and sugar before marinating.
2. In a slow cooker, heat about two tablespoons of sunflower oil and cook the seafood until they turn color.
3. In the remaining one tablespoon of sunflower oil, cook the garlic until fragrant.

4. Place the mushroom and red pepper in the oven for about a half-minute or until soft and mildly seared.
5. Asparagus and winter bean pieces should be added at this stage.
6. Add a pinch of salt to taste.
7. Return the seafood to the pan with the curry powder and sesame oil drizzled on top.
8. Fry quickly and remove from the pan as soon as possible.

3.7 Black Bean Sauce with Stir Fry Veggies

Cooking Time: 30 minutes
Serving Size: 4

Ingredients:
Black Bean Sauce
- 1 tablespoon brown sugar
- 1 teaspoon chili garlic sauce
- 1 tablespoon rice cooking wine
- 1 tablespoon water
- 2 tablespoon garlic sauce

Vegetables
- 2 small zucchini
- 2 bulbs bok choy
- 2 cloves garlic
- ½ large red bell pepper
- 3 tablespoon avocado oil
- 1 large carrot
- 1 teaspoon fresh ginger
- 3 green onions
- 1 large Chinese eggplant

Method:
1. Combine packaged sweet chili sauce, rice cooking liquor, water, coconut milk, and chili garlic sauce in a small cup.
2. Preheat the oven to 350°F and a large pan to a moderate flame.

3. In a flour mixture, combine the eggplant and one tablespoon of oil.
4. In a hot oven skillet, add the eggplant. Sauté until the vegetables are soft and golden brown.
5. Heat the remaining oil in the same pan.
6. Green onion, broccoli, pepper, and garlic are all good additions.
7. Sauté the bell pepper, zucchini, and scallions until soft, stirring occasionally.
8. Return the eggplant to the veggies, stir in the black bean sauce, reduce the heat to low, and continue to cook for a few minutes.
9. Serve over potatoes, Asian noodles, or zoodles while still warm.

3.8 Spring Veggie Stir-Fry

Cooking Time: 20 minutes
Serving Size: 4
  Ingredients:
- Pinch of salt
- ½ bunch thin asparagus
- 1 small red onion
- 3 medium carrots
- ¼ cup soy sauce
- ½ teaspoon red pepper
- 1 tablespoon coconut oil
- 2 tablespoons honey
- 1 tablespoon ginger
- 1 large clove garlic
- 2 teaspoons arrowroot starch

Method:
1. Mix the sesame oil, sugar, cornflour, spice, garlic, and bell pepper flakes in a fluid measuring cup.
2. Preheat oil in a medium saucepan until it shimmers.
3. With a sprinkle of flour, toss in the onion and carrots.

4. Heat, mixing every 30 seconds, till the carrots begin to caramelize, then add the asparagus.
5. Pour in the ready sauce and cook for 30 to 60 seconds, stirring frequently.
6. Remove from the heat and season with salt, fried eggs, or tofu.

3.9 Chinese Cabbage Stir-Fry

Cooking Time: 15 minutes
Serving Size: 4
Ingredients:
- 1 tablespoon soy sauce
- 1 tablespoon Chinese cooking wine
- 2 cloves garlic
- 1 pound cabbage
- 1 tablespoon vegetable oil

Method:
1. In a slow cooker or large pan, heat the peanut oil over medium-high heat.
2. Cook for a few minutes, constantly stirring, before the garlic starts to brown.
3. Close the skillet and continue cooking after stirring in the broccoli until it is fully coated in oil.
4. Continue cooking for the next minute after adding the soy sauce.
5. Mix in the Chinese cooking wine and raise the heat to be heavy.
6. Cook and stir for another two minutes, or until the cabbage is soft.

3.10 Veggie and Tofu Stir-Fry

Cooking Time: 50 minutes
Serving Size: 4
  Ingredients:
  For Tofu
  - ½ teaspoon black pepper
  - 2 tablespoon cornstarch
  - 1 tablespoon soy sauce
  - 1 tablespoon sesame oil
  - 1 (14-oz.) block tofu

  For Stir Fry
  - 1 red bell pepper
  - 2 green onions
  - 2 small carrots
  - 1 small head of broccoli
  - 1 tablespoon ginger
  - 8 oz. string beans
  - Kosher salt
  - 3 cloves garlic
  - 3 tablespoon olive oil

  For Sauce
  - 2 tablespoon packed brown sugar
  - 2 teaspoon cornstarch
  - 2 teaspoon sesame oil
  - ¼ cup water
  - 2 tablespoon l soy sauce

Method:
1. Tofu should be simmered for two minutes in a small saucepan of salted boiling water.
2. Slice tofu into bite-size bits and combine in a mixing saucepan with sesame oil, soy sauce, and garlic powder.
3. In a large frying pan, heat two tablespoons of oil.
4. Allow tofu to fry. Salt and pepper to taste.

5. Cook the ginger and garlic in the leftover one tablespoon oil until aromatic.
6. String beans, broccoli, kale, bell pepper, and fresh basil should all be added at this stage.
7. Heat for 10 minutes, or until the vegetables are tender. Salt and pepper to taste.
8. Combine sesame oil, soy sauce, water, coconut milk, and cornflour in a small cup.
9. Stir and continue cooking, or until moderately thickened.

3.11 Seitan Stir-Fry and Vegan Chinese Vegetable Recipe

Cooking Time: 25 minutes
Serving Size: 4
   Ingredients:
   For the Stir-Fry Sauce
   - 2 teaspoons corn starch
   - ½ tablespoon dark soy sauce
   - 2 teaspoons sesame oil
   - 2 teaspoons maple syrup
   - 1 tablespoon Shaoxing wine
   - 2 tablespoons soy sauce

   For the Stir-Fry
   - 1 medium red pepper
   - 1 medium carrot
   - 4 cloves garlic
   - 1 head broccoli
   - 1 medium red onion
   - 1 portion seitan

Method:
1. To make the sauce, combine all of the ingredients.
2. Preheat a large nonstick skillet. One tablespoon balanced oil of choice.
3. Fry until the seitan is neatly caramelized and crispy around the edges.

4. In the same pan, heat another 12 tablespoons of oil and add the onion, sautéing for 3-4 minutes.
5. Heat for another two minutes after adding the garlic.
6. Combine the lettuce, cabbage, and red pepper in a large mixing bowl.
7. Cook for five minutes, or until the vegetables are tender.
8. Finally, return the seitan to the pot with the stir-fry liquid.
9. Toss until all of the sauce has been dispersed equally.

3.12 Tofu Stir-Fry with Garlic Sauce

Cooking Time: 30 minutes
Serving Size: 4
  Ingredients:
  For the Sauce
- 1 teaspoon sesame oil
- 1 tablespoon cornstarch
- 1 teaspoon ginger
- 2 teaspoons sriracha sauce
- 2 tablespoons water
- 4 garlic cloves
- 2 tablespoons rice vinegar
- 2 tablespoons maple syrup
- ¼ cup soy sauce

For the Tofu Stir-Fry
- 1 medium broccoli crown
- 4 ounces shiitake mushroom
- 3 scallions
- 1 medium carrot
- 1 (14 ounces) package tofu
- 1 tablespoon canola oil

Method:
1. In a small mixing bowl, combine the sauce ingredients.
2. In a skillet, add the tofu squares.
3. Tofu should be cooked for about ten minutes.
4. Move the tofu to a tray after removing it from the pan.
5. Increase the temperature to high.
6. In a skillet, combine the white pieces of the shallots and the carrots.
7. 1 minute of stir-frying.
8. In the same skillet, add the kale and mushrooms. Stir-fry for another two or three minutes.
9. Apply the sauces to the tofu and return it to the pan.
10. Take the pan from the pan and add the scallions' green bits.
11. Serve on plates with sesame oil on top. Serve with a side of rice.

3.13 Chinese Broccoli with Oyster Sauce

Cooking Time: 8 minutes
Serving Size: 2

Ingredients:
- 1 bunch Chinese broccoli

Oyster Sauce
- 1 clove garlic
- 1 teaspoon ginger
- ½ tablespoon vegetable oil
- ½ teaspoon sugar
- 1 tablespoon Chinese cooking wine
- ½ teaspoon sesame oil
- ¾ teaspoon cornflour
- 2 tablespoon oyster sauce
- 2 teaspoon soy sauce
- 3 tablespoon water

Method:
1. Remove the ends of the Chinese Broccoli.
2. Combine liquid and corn starch in a medium bowl, mix to absorb.
3. Then add the rest and bring to the boil on medium heat.
4. Remove from heat after 30 seconds to allow the sauce to stiffen.
5. Serve with a drizzle of sesame oil over Chinese broccoli.
6. It is best served hot.

3.14 Ramen Stir Fry

Cooking Time: 30 minutes
Serving Size: 4
Ingredients:
- 2 green onions
- ½ teaspoon sesame seeds
- 3 cloves garlic
- 1 tablespoon ginger
- 2 (3.5-ounce) ramen noodles
- 1 pound lean beef
- 1 cup diced sweet onion
- 1 teaspoon Sriracha
- 1 tablespoon sesame oil
- ¼ cup oyster sauce
- 1 tablespoon rice wine vinegar
- 1/3 cup beef stock

Method:
1. Stir fry ramen pasta until soft in a big pot of water.
2. Mix vegetable stock, oyster sauce, rice vinegar, and Sriracha in a medium mixing bowl.
3. In a medium saucepan, heat soy sauce over medium-high heat.
4. Cook, occasionally stirring, until the ground beef has golden brown, about 3-5 minutes.

5. One minute after adding the garlic and ginger, mix until aromatic.
6. Scrape any browned bits from the lower part of the skillet before adding the beef stock blend.
7. About 1-2 minutes after adding the ramen noodles, stir until they are heated through it and equitably coated in sauce.
8. Mix thoroughly with spring onions and sesame seeds as a garnish.

3.15 Chinese Fried Rice

Cooking Time: 30 minutes
Serving Size: 4
  Ingredients:
- 3 large eggs
- Thinly sliced green onions
- 2 cloves garlic
- 2 tablespoon soy sauce
- 1 cup rice
- 1 large carrot
- 1 ½ cup frozen peas
- 1 tablespoon. sesame oil
- 1 large onion
- Kosher salt

Method:
1. Take 2 cups of water and brown rice to a boil in a small saucepan.
2. Cover and simmer for 20 minutes, or until all of the water has been absorbed.
3. Fluff with a fork after seasoning with salt.
4. Add the oil to a large frying pan.
5. Cook, occasionally stirring, until the onion, carrot, and peas are tender around 10 to 15 minutes.
6. Cook for another minute until the garlic and soy sauces are fragrant.
7. Scramble the eggs for 1 to 2 minutes.
8. Three minutes after adding the cooked rice, heat thoroughly.
9. Cover with spring onions and rain of sesame oil.

3.16 Cashew Stir Fry Kale Mushroom

Cooking Time: 10 minutes

Serving Size: 2
   Ingredients:
- 1 teaspoon Chinese five-spice
- 1 tablespoon soy sauce
- 1 cup peas
- ¼ cup raw cashew nuts
- 2-3 teaspoons groundnut oil
- 170g mushrooms
- 225g kale
- 1 red chili
- 1 small piece of ginger

Method:
1. In a large nonstick skillet, heat the oil.
2. Combine the ginger, chili, and mushrooms in a bowl.
3. Fry for a total of two minutes.
4. Toss in the kale and lentils. Cook for a total of two minutes.
5. Heat for two minutes after adding the cashews.
6. Toss in the five-spice powder and soy sauce in the pan.
7. Toss with the remaining ingredients, heat through, and serve.

3.17 Vegetables in Hot Garlic Sauce

Cooking Time: 20 minutes
Serving Size: 4
   Ingredients:
   Hot Garlic Sauce
- 1 teaspoon red chili flakes
- ¼ cup red chili sauce
- 1 tablespoon sugar
- 2 tablespoon soy sauce

Vegetables
- 1 cup baby corn
- 1 cup zucchini

- 1 cup red bell pepper
- 1 cup mushrooms
- 1 cup green capsicum
- 1 cup yellow bell pepper
- 1 large-size onion, diced

Other Ingredients
- 2 tablespoon cornflour
- 4 cup water
- Salt to taste
- ½ teaspoon black pepper
- 4 whole dry red chilies
- 2 tablespoon white vinegar
- 4 tablespoon sesame oil
- 1 tablespoon ginger
- 2 tablespoon celery
- Ten garlic cloves
- 2 tablespoon cooking oil

Method:
1. Vegetables should be washed, cleaned, and chopped.
2. ½ cup water to dissolve the cornflour
3. Brown sugar, red chili flakes, sesame oil, and Sriracha sauce should all be combined.
4. In a wok or boil pan, heat the olive oil.
5. Stir-fry all of the veggies, except the onion, for 1 to 2 minutes at medium temperature.
6. In the same skillet, heat soy sauce.
7. Garlic, whole red bell peppers, ginger, and celery, thinly sliced
8. Stir in the diced onion and cook for a few minutes.
9. Pour in the white vinegar and stir well.
10. After that, add the hot garlic seasoning mix that has been prepared.
11. To combine, stir everything together. Salt and black pepper to taste.

12. Add green onions, crushed peanuts, and red chili to the gravy as a garnish.

3.18 Stir-Fried Chinese Egg Noodles with Oyster Sauce

Cooking Time: 20 minutes
Serving Size: 2
  Ingredients:
   - 2 tablespoon vegetable oil
   - To taste black pepper
   - 1 teaspoon sesame oil
   - 1 teaspoon sesame seeds
   - 1 tablespoon soy sauce
   - 1 teaspoon fish sauce
   - 1 package (12.5 oz.) egg noodles
   - 1 large clove garlic
   - 2 tablespoon oyster sauce
   - 6 Brussels sprouts
   - 1/3 cup carrots
   - ½ small onion
   - ½ cup green beans

Method:
1. In a huge nonstick pan or skillet, pour the olive oil and heat it over medium-high heat.
2. After that, combine the Brussels sprouts, parsley, and onion in a mixing bowl.
3. Cook the veggies for 40 seconds on low heat.
4. Green beans and carrots should be added to the pan.
5. Then add the oyster sauce, sesame oil, soy sauce, and fish sauce to the veggies.
6. Cook for the next minute after stirring the vegetables thoroughly.
7. Add the egg noodles to the pot.
8. Remove the stir-fried Chinese rice noodles and veggies from the wok and place them in large bowls.

Chapter 4: Vegetarian Wok Thai Recipes

4.1 Thai Stir-Fried Vegetables with Garlic, Ginger, and Lime

Cooking Time: 20 minutes
Serving Size: 6

Ingredients:
- Fresh coriander
- Cashew nuts
- Baby corn
- Sesame oil
- Bamboo shoots
- Water chestnuts
- 1 red capsicum
- 3 cups bok choy
- 6 shiitake mushrooms
- 1 small head of broccoli
- ¼ cup shallots
- 1 fresh chili
- 1 carrot, sliced
- 2 thumb size ginger
- 6 cloves garlic

Stir-Fry Sauce
- ½ teaspoon dry chili flakes
- 2½ teaspoons brown sugar
- 3½ tablespoons lime juice
- 1½ tablespoons soy sauce
- 2½ tablespoons fish sauce
- 400ml coconut milk

Method:
1. In a cup or pan, mix all of the components for the stir fry sauce.
2. To remove the sugar, stir vigorously.

3. In a hot wok, pour in the oil.
4. Combine the shallot, garlic, ginger, and chili in a large mixing bowl.
5. Add the carrots and mushrooms, as well as a quarter of the sauce mixture.
6. ½ of the remaining sauce, tomatoes, bell pepper, and bamboo shoots
7. Insert the bok choy and as well as residual sauce.
8. Wrap up the dish with a generous sprinkling of cashew nuts.

4.2 Thai Stir-Fried Mixed Vegetables Recipe

Cooking Time: 40 minutes
Serving Size: 4
  Ingredients:
  - Thai chilies
  - 1 teaspoon sugar
  - 5 shiitake mushrooms
  - 5 cloves garlic
  - 3 stalks Chinese broccoli
  - 10 sugar snap peas
  - 2 tablespoon oyster sauce
  - ¼ head cauliflower
  - 3 cups cabbage
  - 2 teaspoon soy sauce
  - 1 tablespoon water
  - ½ cup carrots
  - 2 teaspoon golden mountain sauce

Method:
1. Combine oyster sauce, sesame oil, golden mountains seasoning, and water in a small cup.
2. Combine the carrot and cabbage in a mixing dish.
3. Later, add the cabbage, snap beans, gai lan roots, and mushroom.
4. Switch the medium heat in a skillet or a big sauté pan, insert a little vegetable oil, onions, bell peppers, and sauté.
5. Toss in the carrots and cauliflower for around two minutes over medium heat.
6. Insert bowl 2 of veggies.
7. Toss until the veggies are almost completed to your taste.
8. Add gai lan leaf, toss just until softened.

4.3 Vegetarian Thai Noodles

Cooking Time: 15 minutes
Serving Size: 4
   Ingredients:
   For the Pad Thai
- ½ cup peanuts
- ½ cup fresh herbs
- 2 tablespoons oil
- 1 egg, beaten
- 4 ounces brown rice noodles
- Half a yellow onion
- 2 carrots
- 1 red pepper
- 1 zucchini

For the Sauce
- 1 tablespoon soy sauce
- 1 teaspoon chili paste
- 3 tablespoons vegetable broth
- 2 tablespoons white vinegar
- 3 tablespoons brown sugar
- 3 tablespoons fish sauce

Method:
1. To soak the undercooked noodles, place them in a bowl of ice water.
2. In a pan, mix the sauce ingredients and shake well.
3. Over medium-high pressure, heat a tablespoon of oil.
4. Stir in the vegetables and cook for a few minutes.
5. Add a further tablespoon of oil to a pan.
6. Add the pasta to the hot pan and stir fry for just a moment, using tweezers to toss.
7. Mix in the liquid for another couple of minutes, just until the sauce begins to thicken and adhere to the noodles.

8. With both the tongs, flip it around. The egg combination will cling to the noodles, causing them to become sticky.
9. Remove from heat after adding the veggies and tossing them together.

4.4 Easy Thai Basil Vegetable Stir Fry

Cooking Time: 25 minutes
Serving Size: 4
Ingredients:
- 3 carrots
- 3 cups Thai basil
- 1 bell pepper
- 2 cups snap peas
- 1 cup uncooked rice
- 2 tablespoon coconut oil
- 1 head broccoli
- 3 large garlic cloves

For the Sauce
- ½ teaspoon sesame oil
- 1 tablespoon coconut sugar
- 1 tablespoon fish sauce
- 2 tablespoon rice vinegar
- 2 tablespoon tamari

Method:
1. Cook rice according to package directions and set aside.
2. Mix all seasoning ingredients in a small bowl and set aside.
3. Melt the coconut oil in a large saucepan over medium heat.
4. Add garlic and simmer for one moment.
5. It should turn a golden brown color but not burn. Keep a close eye on things.
6. Broccoli, red pepper, peas, and vegetables are all good additions.
7. Enable 3 minutes for the vegetables to steam.

8. Stir in the basil and cook for another 1-2 minutes, or until the basil has wilted.

4.5 Spicy Thai Basil Fried Rice

Cooking Time: 40 minutes
Serving Size: 6
Ingredients:
- 1 cucumber
- ½ cup cilantro sprigs
- 1 onion
- 2 cups sweet Thai basil
- 1 red pepper
- 6 large cloves garlic clove
- 2 serrano peppers
- 3 tablespoons oyster sauce
- ½ cup peanut oil
- 4 cups jasmine rice
- 1 teaspoon white sugar
- 2 tablespoons fish sauce

Method:
1. In a mixing bowl, combine the oyster sauce, shrimp paste, and sugar.
2. In a skillet, add the oil over a moderate flame until it begins to start smoking.
3. Add the onion and chilies peppers, mixing quickly.
4. Mix in the green pepper, onion, and oyster sauce combination; cook.
5. Boost the heat to maximum and rapidly stir in the cooled rice, blending the sauce into the rice.
6. Remove the pan from the heat and add the spring onions.
7. As needed, garnish with shredded cabbage and coriander.

4.6 Thai Vegetable Fried Rice with Cashews

Cooking Time: 30 minutes
Serving Size: 6
  Ingredients:
- ½ lime
- 2 tablespoon Thai basil
- 4 cup broccoli florets
- 1 cup sweet peas frozen
- 1 tablespoon brown sugar
- 4 cup jasmine rice
- 1 cup cashews
- 4 tablespoon tamari divided
- 2 tablespoon liquid amino
- 5 tablespoon sesame oil
- 1 tablespoon fresh ginger
- 2 teaspoon red chili pepper flakes
- 1½ cup yellow onion
- 1 cup red bell pepper
- 1 tablespoon fresh garlic
- 1 cup shiitake

Method:
1. Heat the oven to 350F. In a cookie sheet, put the cashews and cook for 12-14 minutes.
2. Warm the sesame oil in a big Dutch oven until it shimmers.
3. Add the mushrooms to the vegetables and stir fry for two minutes.
4. Mix in the bell peppers with the mushrooms and vegetables for another two minutes.
5. On medium-low heat, add the onion, spice, and red pepper flakes to the vegetables' combination and cook for one minute.
6. Transfer the broccoli and green peas to the rice combination.

7. Stir until all of the vegetables are distributed equally.
8. Place the rice in large bowls and top with green onions, sesame seeds, additional herbs, and lime sliders.

4.7 Vegetarian Thai Yellow Curry

Cooking Time: 30 minutes
Serving Size: 4
Ingredients:
Curry
- ¼ cup roasted cashews
- 1 medium lemon
- ¼ cup green peas
- 2 ripe mangos
- 1 ½ tablespoon coconut oil
- 1 teaspoon ground turmeric
- 1 red bell pepper
- 1 medium shallot
- ¼ teaspoon sea salt
- 2-3 teaspoon tamari
- 2 tablespoon fresh ginger
- 2 14-ounce coconut milk
- 3 tablespoon coconut sugar
- 2 cloves minced garlic
- 1 cup chopped red cabbage
- 3 tablespoon red curry paste
- 1 Thai red chili

Method:
1. Over medium-high heat, heat a big cast-iron skillet.
2. Add the coconut oil, red onion, carrot, cloves, and peppers once the pan is warmed.
3. Add a pinch of salt and cook, constantly stirring, for three minutes.

4. Stir in the cabbage and red curry spice, and bake for another two minutes.
5. Stir in coconut milk, maple syrup, sea salt, soya sauce, and turmeric.
6. Reduce heat to low and add bell pepper and peas.
7. Heat, stirring periodically, for 5-ten minutes to soften the peppers and peas and incorporate them with curry flavor.
8. After the broth has been well-seasoned and the peppers have lightened, add the mango, cashew nuts, and lime juice and continue to cook for 3-4 minutes.
9. Serve with steamed broccoli and rice or coconut brown rice.

4.8 Thai Satay Stir-Fry

Cooking Time: 10 minutes
Serving Size: 4

Ingredients:
- Handful basil leaves
- 25g roasted peanuts
- Thumb-sized root ginger
- 300g pack stir-fry vegetable
- 300g pack noodle
- 1 tablespoon oil
- 3 tablespoon sweet chili sauce
- 2 tablespoon soy sauce
- 3 tablespoon peanut butter

Method:
1. To form a delicious satay sauce, combine the peanut butter, chili sauce, water, and sesame oil.
2. Place the pasta in a bowl and cover it with boiling water.
3. To detach, softly stir, then wash completely.
4. In a skillet, heat the oil, then whisk the herb and the tougher vegetables.

5. Stir in the pasta and the remaining vegetables for 1-2 minutes over medium temperature or until the veggies are just fried.
6. Place the vegetables on one side of the pan and the bean paste on the other.
7. Bring the water to a boil. To serve, combine the sauce with the stir-fry, then top with spring onions and peanuts.

4.9 Vegetarian Pad See Ew with Tofu and Chinese Eggplant

Cooking Time: 30 minutes
Serving Size: 4
Ingredients:
- 12 oz. broccoli
- 2 large eggs, beaten
- 2 cloves garlic
- 1 tablespoon water
- 3 tablespoons canola oil
- 1/3 cup shallot
- 2 tablespoons dark soy sauce
- 16 oz. extra firm tofu
- 1 lb. rice noodle
- 1 tablespoon light brown sugar
- 1 teaspoon Thai chili powder
- 3 tablespoons oyster sauce

Method:
1. Mix the sesame oil, vegan oyster sauce, coconut milk, and chili powder in a small cup.
2. Drizzle 2 teaspoons of the sauce over the tofu in a medium dish.
3. In a wide nonstick skillet, heat two tablespoons of oil, circling the pot to coat it.
4. In the same pan, add the rest tablespoon of olive oil.
5. Heat until the shallots are soft and golden brown in the pan.

6. Heat for thirty seconds, or until the garlic and water are fragrant.
7. Heat, sometimes tossing, until the Chinese broccoli is tender.
8. Toss in the stored rice noodles, tofu, and sauces until all is well combined.
9. Toss the eggs with the rest of the ingredients to combine them.

4.10 Veggie Thai Red Curry

Cooking Time: 20 minutes
Serving Size: 4

Ingredients:
- 1 teaspoon brown sugar
- Jasmine rice
- 140g sugar snap pea
- 20g pack basil
- ½ red pepper
- 140g mushrooms
- 200g firm tofu, cubed
- 1 courgette
- 1 small aubergine
- 2 tablespoon vegetable oil
- 400ml can coconut milk
- Juice 3 limes
- 2 red chilies
- 4-5 tablespoon soy sauce

For the Paste
- 1 teaspoon pepper
- 1 teaspoon ground coriander
- Thumb-size piece ginger
- 2 garlic cloves
- Zest 1 lime
- Stalks coriander
- 3 red chilies
- 3 shallots

- ½ red pepper
- 1 lemongrass

Method:
1. In a mixing bowl, combine the paste components.
2. Toss the tofu with two tablespoons of sesame oil, one lemon juice, and chopped chili.
3. In a wide pan, heat half of the oil. Fry 3-4 tablespoons of paste.
4. Cook for ten minutes after adding the cocoa powder, water, aubergine, courgette, and pepper.
5. Drain the tofu, pat it dry, and then fry it until crispy in a shallow saucepan with the cooking liquid.
6. Toss in the onions, sugar snap peas, and the majority of the herbs.
7. Cook until the mushrooms are soft, about three minutes.
8. Serve with rice noodles and garnished with sliced chili and basil.

4.11 Easy Vegetable Stir Fry with Creamy Peanut Sauce

Cooking Time: 25 minutes
Serving Size: 2

Ingredients:

For the Peanut Sauce
- ¼ cup water
- 1 tablespoon maple syrup
- 2 tablespoon soy sauce
- 2 tablespoon sweet chili sauce
- 2 tablespoon peanut butter

For the Stir-Fry
- 3.5 oz. noodles
- 1 handful peanuts
- 1 big handful of snow peas
- 6-8 baby corns
- 1 tablespoon peanut oil

- 1 onion
- 2-3 cups vegetables
- 1 piece ginger
- 1 clove garlic

Method:
1. Gather all of the ingredients and place them in one location.
2. Put the peanut butter, sesame oil, sweet chili sauce, liquid, and syrup in a large mixing bowl.
3. Then use a spoon, thoroughly combine the ingredients.
4. Prepare the noodles.
5. Add the oil in a sauté pan or large skillet until it begins to smoke.
6. Combine the garlic, spice, onion, candy snaps, and green beans in a large mixing bowl.
7. After about 40 seconds, add the defrosted vegetables.
8. For around 4-5 minutes, vigorously stir it.
9. Reduce the heat to medium-low and stir in the sauce and pasta.
10. Check to see if everything is smooth and creamy.
11. Allow for another 3-5 minutes of simmering.
12. Before eating, remove the thyme.

4.12 Thai Morning Glory Stir Fry

Cooking Time: 5 minutes
Serving Size: 4
Ingredients:
- ½ tablespoon oyster sauce
- 1 tablespoon vegetable oil
- ½ tablespoon soybean paste
- ½ tablespoon soy sauce
- 4 Thai hot chili
- 3 large cloves of garlic
- 1 bunch water morning glory

Method:
1. Put the morning glory in a container and break it into 4 inch long parts.
2. Then weigh the sauce ingredients and add them to the bowl as well.
3. Add the garlic and bell peppers to the edge of the dish, broken up.
4. In a large skillet, add the oil until it is very warm, then insert the container's components all at once.
5. Mix and fry rapidly till the morning glory is softened, having to turn for the lower part.

4.13 Thai Combination Fried Rice

Cooking Time: 20 minutes
Serving Size: 4
Ingredients:
- 2 eggs
- 3 cups cooked jasmine rice
- 5 oz. prawns
- 3 green onion
- 2 large garlic cloves
- ½ onion

- 2 tablespoon vegetable oil

Method:
1. In a wide skillet or a big pan, heat the oil over medium-low heat.
2. Stir in the garlic and onion for thirty seconds.
3. Stir in the prawns and the white part of the spring onion for two minutes.
4. Push all aside and pour the eggs on the opposite side. It should only take about 20 seconds to scramble it.
5. Toss in the rice and your favorite sauce.
6. Stir fry for two minutes, halfway through incorporating the green portion of the bell peppers.
7. Mix thoroughly with fresh coriander on top and tomatoes and cucumbers on the bottom.

4.14 Vegetarian Pad Thai with Zoodles

Cooking Time: 25 minutes
Serving Size: 2

Ingredients:

For The Sauce
- 1 tablespoon honey
- 1-3 teaspoons chili garlic sauce
- 1½ tablespoons rice vinegar
- 1 tablespoon soy sauce
- 2 tablespoons fish sauce

For the Vegetarian Pad Thai
- ¼ cup fresh cilantro
- Lime wedges for serving
- 2 large green onions
- ¼ cup peanuts
- 1 cup carrots
- ½ cup shelled edamame
- 2 large eggs
- 1 cup bean sprouts
- 2 medium zucchini

- 2 cloves garlic
- 1 teaspoon olive oil

Method:
1. In a shallow saucepan, stir together all the sauce components.
2. Slice the zucchini into zoodles using a spiralizer.
3. In a large skillet over medium heat or broiler, heat one teaspoon of butter over medium-low heat.
4. After the garlic has been added, smash the eggs into the pan.
5. Break the yolk apart like a spoon and simmer for thirty seconds or until it just starts to settle.
6. Stir in the pasta and sauce to combine.
7. Add the green beans, broccoli, edamame, and sliced spring onions and bake till the bean sprouts are crisp-tender, about five minutes.
8. Toss in the coriander and nuts.

4.15 Thai Stir-Fry with Coconut Rice

Cooking Time: 25 minutes
Serving Size: 4

Ingredients:
Coconut Rice
- 1 teaspoon sugar
- 1 pinch salt
- 1 can Thai Coconut Milk
- 1 ¼ cups water
- 1 ½ cups jasmine rice

Thai Vegetables Stir-Fry
- 1 medium red bell pepper
- 1 small onion
- 2 tablespoons vegetable oil
- 2 cups snow peas
- 1 pound vegetables
- ½ teaspoon garlic powder
- ¼ teaspoon red pepper
- 3 tablespoons flour
- ¼ cup soy sauce
- 1 teaspoon ground ginger
- ¼ cup honey
- 1 cup vegetable stock

Method:
1. Wash jasmine rice with liquid.
2. Bring canola oil, liquid, salt, and sugar to simmer in a small saucepan on a moderate flame.
3. Return to a boil with the rice.
4. In a medium mixing bowl, coat the veggies in flour.
5. In a separate bowl, mix the residual flour, stocks, sugar, sesame oil, garlic, garlic powder, and red pepper; whisk until soft.

6. In a wok or broad skillet over medium-high heat, heat one tablespoon of the oil. Toss in some fruits.
7. In a skillet, heat the remaining one tablespoon of oil.
8. Offer with Coconut Rice on the side.

4.16 Thai Green Curry with Homemade Curry Paste

Cooking Time: 30 minutes
Serving Size: 6
Ingredients:
- 2 teaspoon Thai fish sauce
- 3 tablespoon olive oil
- 1 teaspoon ground cumin
- 1 teaspoon black peppercorns
- 8 kaffir lime leaves
- 1 tablespoon coriander seeds
- 4-6 medium green chilies
- 2 lemongrass stalks
- 1 lime
- 2 shallots
- 2 garlic cloves
- Small bunch coriander
- 5cm fresh ginger

Method:
1. Stir fry ingredients. Put all of the food items in a mixing bowl and blitz to a mixture.
2. Use right away or hold in the refrigerator for up to three days in a jar.

4.17 Rainbow Vegetarian Pad Thai with Crispy Noodles

Cooking Time: 30 minutes
Serving Size: 4
Ingredients:
Noodles
- 1 carrot
- 1 tablespoon sesame oil
- 1 yellow capsicum

- 1 brown onion
- 1 green zucchini
- 1 red capsicum
- 250g Thai style rice noodles

Sauce
- 1 teaspoon fish sauce
- 1 teaspoon sriracha chili sauce
- 1 tablespoon rice vinegar
- 1 tablespoon maple syrup
- 3 tablespoon soy sauce

Garnish
- 1 packet fried noodles
- Juice of 1 lime
- 3 green onions

Method:
1. Prepare the noodles as directed on the package.
2. To make the sauce, mix all of the components in a mixing bowl.
3. Add the soy sauce and onions to the skillet and stir fry for two minutes, then add the vegetables and capsicums and stir fry for another two minutes.
4. Finally, mix in the zucchini for just one minute.
5. Place the cooked noodles in the skillet and pour the sauce over them.
6. Return the veggies to the skillet. Merge the noodles with the sauce.
7. Remove from heat and garnish with spring onions, lemon juice, and fried noodles.
8. Combine all ingredients and serve right away.

Conclusion

During the wok heating process, the intense temperature of the pan sears the veggies. Their colors appear even clearer and more vivid as a result of this. As a response, wok-cooked meals are often very attractive. On the other hand, deep-frying causes the food to lose its color or become burnt, making it seem less appetizing. For their masterful use of veggies, meats, and fish with reasonable saturated fat and liquids that are not too rich, wok cooking and Chinese food have been promoted as safe and attractive, provided calories are maintained at an acceptable amount. Wok cooking is a nutritious and fast way to prepare a wide range of dishes. Try the wok recipes in the "vegetarian wok cookbook" with wok recipes from Asian countries and prepare healthy vegetarian meals.

Printed in Great Britain
by Amazon